Still the Hunger

Beverley Hutton

Foreword by Chris Gore

[16]I pray that out of his glorious riches he may strengthen you with power through his Spirit in your inner being, [17]so that Christ may dwell in your hearts through faith. And I pray that you, being rooted and established in love, [18]may have power, together with all the Lord's holy people, to grasp how wide and long and high and deep is the love of Christ, [19]and to know this love that surpasses knowledge- that you may be filled to the measure of all the fullness of God. Ephesians 3:16–19 (NIV)

*For Paul, Nicholas, and Jonathon
Let my love continuously nourish your hearts.
My purpose for telling you these things is so that the joy
that I experience will fill your hearts with overflowing
gladness.* (John 15:9,11)

Contents

Foreword	Chris Gore	vii
Introduction		ix
Chapter 1	Evie 2004	1
Chapter 2	The Oak Unit 1987	7
Chapter 3	The Presenting Past 2004	17
Chapter 4	The Blue Room 1971	23
Chapter 5	Hungry 1979	35
Chapter 6	Though She May Forget, I Will Not Forget You	41
Chapter 7	Runaway 1981	45
Chapter 8	Car Crash	63
Chapter 9	Punishment/Reward I	71
Chapter 10	The Goldfish Bowl	99
Chapter 11	Punishment/Reward II	107
Chapter 12	New Beginnings	117
Chapter 13	Blessings	125
Chapter 14	The Prince of Peace	129
Chapter 15	Staying in a Place of Peace	135
Chapter 16	Stilling the Hunger in Others	143
Chapter 17	Integrating Therapy, Healing and Discipleship	151
Chapter 18	Faulty Perspectives	155
Chapter 19	Forty Years	165
Acknowledgements		175
MORE		177
References		178

Foreword

Imagine with me for a moment a life filled with extreme trauma, pain, darkness, and hopelessness: a life with no apparent answers, no one to turn to, alone and abandoned. And then in a moment of time, freedom comes. Unlike anything you've experienced before, simple and complete…freedom in its purest form, Jesus reaching down and pulling you from the pit of pain. Life beautifully restored, full of joy, love, and passion once again.

This is the story of Beverley Hutton and while she experienced things I wish no one on earth ever had to experience, I love that Jesus gets the final say in her story. I love that hope can arise in every situation and that no matter what we face, Jesus is bigger still. He is the answer to every problem, every pain-filled body, and every aching heart.

I admire Beverley and how she was able to keep her eyes on Jesus, through the heartache and trials. While we don't understand why breakthrough doesn't always come immediately, we know there is a peace accessible to us in the midst of our circumstances, a peace that passes all understanding. Beverley has come to experience that peace first-hand.

As the Director of Bethel Healing ministries, it's my passion to see people set free from sickness, pain, and disease. This is why I would encourage you with Beverley's story. If Jesus did it for her, He wants to do it for you too. Nothing is impossible, no situation or circumstance is too big for Him. No life is hopeless. He is bigger still. I pray that as you read Beverley's story, you will come face to face with the Answer, Jesus. He is abounding with hope and is able to dispel all pain, fear, trauma, disease, and hopelessness. May you encounter Him and experience the same freedom Beverley has experienced. May you be filled with the expectant hope that with God nothing is impossible! And may you experience the Shalom peace of God in your life…the peace that dispels all chaos.

Chris Gore
Director of Bethel Healing Ministries
Author "Walking in Supernatural Healing Power"
Redding, California

Introduction

Can God still the hunger for more?

Can God really meet the unmet needs of those who have been so unloved, neglected or harmed by past experiences that they have no idea what love is anymore? Can God's love *ever* be enough for them? Is it possible to forgive the harm done, and to ever walk free of complex trauma? Is it possible for God to fill the emptiness, desires, and longings left by past experiences that people so desperately strive for, unsuccessfully trying to fill with food (or the lack of), or addictions, or the overwhelming compulsion to find an alternative parental figure with whom they inappropriately attach themselves to?

The answer to each of these questions is, "Yes!". I hope that by sharing my own story, along with a mixture of psychoanalytic theory and the word of God, I can show you how to walk in freedom from complex mental health difficulties, such as those as a consequence of severe trauma, neglect, and abuse, and to be able to see yourself as God sees you—precious, safe, and pure. I am a psychodynamic and EMDR (Eye Movement Desensitisation Reprocessing) psychotherapist, as well as the Founder of the mental health charity, Still the Hunger. I've written this book to accompany our course, MORE, which I've written as a resource for the church to assist in understanding complex mental health issues from a Christian perspective.

With ever-growing waiting lists, and the lack of available resources, the church needs to rise up and meet the needs of those who are hurting within our midst. There is a cultural change occurring with a new generation of people coming forwards and speaking out about historical abuse and post-traumatic stress disorder. We need to be equipped to hear, not to turn away and ignore what was previously too hard to think about. Hurting people, who have never been heard or understood, will learn to deal with their pain in a variety of ways. Sometimes it will be expressed as a physical pain, other times it may manifest in a variety of coping mechanisms that are aimed at distracting themselves away from what is too much to bear. Those coping mechanisms can be hard for others to witness and to understand, and may in themselves, cause a repeat of the historical defensive response to turn away from what we suspect, creating a typical and familiar repetition, and confirmation, that nobody cares.

I believe it is essential to look at healing from a combined psychological, physical, and spiritual perspective, instead of separating each of these areas and trying to deal with a complex problem from only one perspective. We were created as physical, emotional, and spiritual beings and I believe that God sees whole people, who are hurting. He heals in a variety of ways regardless of how a problem is manifesting. In the Bible we see Jesus laying hands on the sick, applying mud to eyes, casting out demons, giving instructions to wash in the river, and forgiving sins, regardless of what the problem was. As God works supernaturally to bring about healing into each of these areas of our lives, so we need to work also in partnership with Him, in tune with His word. I believe that therein lies all we need to be able to walk free, but sometimes it takes time and patience for those so severely damaged by complex trauma and abuse.

My accompanying book, *MORE,* is a discipleship course that has been developed through working with so many others at Still the Hunger, and I hope it will enable those so deeply wounded by life to take hold of the fact that they are loved and significant children of God, able to walk in the safety of that knowledge for the rest of their lives, regardless of what they have been through.

It is entirely possible for those with complex mental health difficulties to be able to break free from dysfunctional patterns of relating, and to be able to renew their minds from everything in the past that may have told them that they were worthless, unheard, and unlovable. I hope this book will help you to identify your own negative patterns of thinking and behaviour and help you to think about how you can do something about it. Whilst it is not meant to be triggering, it does not gloss over the reality of what we are often dealing with here, and you may need support from a therapist as you work through this material.

This is essentially what the Still the Hunger charity was set up to do in 2012—to provide a clinical model that integrates discipleship and healing with therapy. Whilst this book will give you some tools to challenge your own coping mechanisms, I am not suggesting that a book or an 8-week course are sufficient, as ongoing therapy is an important part of the Still the Hunger process. However, the material within the

MORE course should enable you to get more out of therapy and help fast-track the process of recovery.

I have sought to tell this story as if during the process of long-term therapy, as so many stories are told by our clients, as well as from the perspective of demonstrating what it can feel like to be dragged backwards and forwards through time by traumatic flashbacks. It is painful and disturbing to look back over this now but makes me ever more grateful for the healing and transformation I have experienced. I have sought to write this in such a way that helps the reader understand the mindset of Dissociative Identity Disorder, Anorexia Nervosa, and Complex Post-traumatic Stress Disorder. If you are suffering yourself, then you will no doubt identify with what I write, but I hope that this gives you hope to believe that nothing is too difficult for God

Our name Still the Hunger comes from Psalm 17:14 'You still the hunger of those you cherish;' in the NIV translation, published by Hodder & Stoughton, 2000 edition. This translation of the psalm sees God blessing the righteous, His treasured ones. He can be trusted to satisfy every need of those He loves.

*Some of the personal details in clinical material used have been changed to maintain client confidentiality.

*Scripture references are taken from a variety of translations throughout, with the version specified.

*This book uses some material originally published in Blue Room.

CHAPTER 1

Evie 2004

I WOKE WITH A START. The atmosphere in the room was icy. Before there was time to contemplate the temperature drop, a brute force pushed me down. What was happening to me? Was I going to die? The pain tore through every part of my body and mind. I prayed as I fought to breathe.

"Mummy! Mummy! Help me!" A little voice cried out from somewhere deep inside my mind, but went unanswered.

Silence filled the room. Had he really gone? I lay still. I wanted to scream but I lay in silence.

"Mummy! I want my mummy!" I curled up in a ball and, as the world faded away, all I could hear was the little girl continuing to cry out for her mummy. Desperate cries to be rescued reverberated around the room and through every part of my mind. And nobody came.

I had made the choice to believe everything that God said about me was true. I knew that I was a precious, loved, child of God. I knew that He had a plan for my life. I knew that as a mother loves a daughter, I would be comforted, and I knew that He would complete the good work He had begun in me. So why was this happening to me?

I could hear a child's voice, but what did it mean, and why now? All had been going well, but there was no denying the fact that I was experiencing something that I hadn't been aware of before. How did I renew my mind and walk in freedom whilst suffering with what appeared to be evidence of a fragmented mind, with dissociated parts that chose to believe their own truth—a truth separated from everything else I knew and linked only to the memory that each specific part carried? I was familiar with Dissociative Identity Disorder (DID), but it had never occurred to me that I might have this problem.

I was to discover a child part, Evie, who was three years old, and needed her mummy to rescue her. Evie appeared to be triggered by feelings of shame, humiliation, physical body memories, and an intense fear that I couldn't comprehend. This internal conflict seemed beyond explanation and completely different to anything I'd encountered so far. The battle to renew my mind and choose truth on the part of 'somebody else' trapped within me, who held information and experiences about my past that I wasn't yet aware of, was inexplicably hard and frustrating. I could still choose to believe the truth that God would complete the good work He had begun in me, and that He is a God who heals, and I clung to that and claimed it over myself and every part of me.

"MUMMY, HELP ME!" I curled up in a ball as my surroundings faded away. "Mummy! Mummy!" I was annoyed with that little girl. "Will you shut up?" I answered curtly. "There's no point calling for her because she never comes anyway."

"I want my mummy!" the voice cried endlessly nevertheless, until I drifted back into sleep.

Then I was dreaming. I was only little, and I was being held down by things I couldn't see. I knew what was about to happen and I knew it was going to hurt. I began to cry. I screamed for my mummy, but she didn't come.

When Evie took over, she was paralysed with fear over something I knew nothing of, and intense feelings of hopelessness, despair, and an overwhelming need to run would kick in. I wouldn't be aware of what the triggers were but would be left to deal with emotions that seemed unconnected to anything else going on in my life moments before. I was fighting to keep my head above water, whilst also fighting to hide it from everyone else—such a common aspect of DID.

The mind splits in order to keep secrets from itself, to hide intolerable situations in order to survive. The 'host' personality, or 'me' if you like (although all of it is me), could continue to go to school and enjoy family holidays, oblivious to what another part of me was having to endure. The other parts were brave, created by my mind without my knowledge, for certain activities or feelings. Each part continued to exist in the moment of their creation and purpose, bringing the past into the present, where it made no sense. I had no idea whatsoever what had happened to them—to me—in order for my mind to fragment, but I knew how DID was created and what it meant, and it was terrifying.

I heard Evie's cries throughout every part of me, grating through my very soul, but nothing reached her. Why doesn't anybody come for this poor child and sort this mess out? Why has she been left alone to suffer like this? I longed to sweep her up within myself, absorb her pain within my own, but I couldn't reach her, for she was trapped within a cage of her own making. A cage of invisible silver strands, fencing her in from every angle, within my own mind. There was no escape, despite having put herself there. I put her there because I couldn't bear to see what happened to me and I split it off from the rest of me and my mind created Evie to bear it all. Evie wasn't alone either—soon I would discover there were others.

Breaking through my thoughts come her cries again. Please make her stop, make this stop, for this shouldn't be happening; not now. I cannot bear listening. Who is the mother she longs to find? She doesn't even exist! Meanwhile, wherever I go, I hear her: through the running water while I shower, on the train, in the car, breaking through my sleep. I hear her haunted cries everywhere I go, but I cannot save her. She has my mind in her hands and I cannot do anything, no matter how much I want this to stop.

For a brief moment, she draws me into herself and I feel her overwhelming terror, like an electric shock upon my skin. Dear God, get me out away from here! What happened to her to make her feel like that? I shut the door behind me in a mad rush for the safety of myself. Whoever could feel like that? "You poor child! I swear I cannot help you!"

Of course, this is how it all began. I had slammed the door shut and blocked it all out many years ago, but now it was bursting out.

"Do something!" I pleaded with God. "What is wrong with her? Surely you can make her talk!" "Sssh," He said with a finger to His lips. "Be still and know who I am."

"You told me that you love me with an everlasting love; that you will rebuild me; that I will dance with joy again, (Jeremiah 31:3–4) but I'm not feeling joy right now. And despite telling me that Your word is living and active, sharper than any double-edged sword, that penetrates even to dividing soul and spirit, joints and marrow, (Hebrews 4:12) and certainly sharper than any blade she wields, and any lies she's listening to that say she can't be loved, I'm not seeing results!"

But His words are true—I know that, and so I claim those words for her as well. I would stand in the gap for her until she could stand and claim them for herself. I had no idea how long I would have to do this for her or whether I would ever be free of this.

Free. Hmm. I already knew that Jesus died so I could be free, and that freedom had already been given. Not feeling it was not an indication that it hadn't been given, or that I had done anything wrong to reverse it. No, the freedom had been given (past tense—see Galatians 5:1) so I chose to stand firm on that truth and claim it, knowing one day my feelings would line up with truth. That knowledge gave me the hope and determination to keep going.

Her cries escape and break my heart as they break through my mind. I call upon God, as only He holds a key to the cage of my making. She recognises Him this time as He bends down to wrap His arms around her. She flings her arms around His neck and cries while I watch from a safe distance, envious of His warm embrace, for I am so needy for His love. I've never known such love as sweet as His. Oh, what love! I can taste Him upon my lips, His perfume fills my lungs as I breathe Him in. I want so much more of Him.

His words didn't reach Evie, though. Her voice cried out for help repeatedly, triggered by memories and what seemed, at times, the most inconsequential thoughts and occurrences. Why I couldn't stop her cries and why she persisted, I didn't know. I had no idea of the cause or how to stop it, and nobody else seemed to either. A fleeting thought about something only vaguely disturbing or shameful and my mind would be taken over by somebody else, this child who desperately wanted her mummy. As the voice shattered through the random thoughts of a few moments earlier, I was startled yet again by her sudden emergence into my life. I tried to ask questions but got nowhere.

"So, who are you? And what do you want from me, because I'm as sure as can be that I can't help you. What happened to you? Who are you?" I pleaded. I sat, holding my head in my hands, not knowing what to do with myself. My head! It feels like it's going to explode, not in pain but from all these thoughts confusing me and leaving me feeling exhausted with all these voices. I have to do something to make sense of this and make it stop but I don't even know where to start. I can't remember anymore. What I did remember seemed bad enough, I thought, so why was this happening when I'd resolved everything? I thought back to when it started.

A very dear friend, Joanie, had just died, which had been a massive loss. For a relatively brief period in my life, she had felt like a mother to me. I had returned to work in the NHS while our sons, Nicholas and Jonathon, completed GCSEs and A levels, resolving to pick up with the vision again when the boys finished school. I had been a medical secretary previously, so I had assumed it easy to return to this. Whilst in the past I had suffered with an understandable fear of doctors, I doubted this would cause me problems now, but I had been wrong.

So, there I was, having just lost somebody who had finally shown me what it was like to feel loved, feeling like a failure, exhausted, and surrounded by doctors all over again. And I crashed. I think I was a good medical secretary, but I simply couldn't work alongside doctors when they triggered flashbacks. I became convinced that they would see through me to the past I couldn't forget. How could I hide any of it when I felt as if I wore it as a neon sign on my forehead? The flashbacks came hard and I stopped eating. Despite my amazement at what was happening, I became incredibly depressed and suddenly I was right back where I had been 20 years earlier. But, beyond the obvious triggers, why I had crashed I didn't know.

> *'My head! I want to cry but I can't. If only I could escape. Get out of this trap. My own mind seems to have built up a huge cage around me that I cannot get through. I feel so distant, and my head is very heavy. I'm so slow and far away. I don't care about anything. I feel trapped and I can't get out of here.'*

Chapter 2

The Oak Unit 1987

THE ROOM WAS DARK and dingy; no lights and only one tiny window near the ceiling, which offered nothing of life outside. I had only minutes, perhaps just seconds, to achieve what I had run in there to do. Slamming and locking the cubicle door behind me, I sat down on the toilet and reached for the razor blade that I had hidden.

I began to cut frantically at my wrist. Tears were streaming down my face, but I felt no pain. As I cut through the first layers of skin, I fought to ignore the globules of fat that repulsed me. I had to work quickly because I knew that I would soon be missed from the day room and swiftly located. Within seconds, blood was pouring on to the floor and spreading out under the cubicle door and, as it flowed, I began to experience relief at last from all my anguish and torment. With those first cuts my mind focused on the hatred I felt directed at myself—at all the frustration that nobody understood or cared. But even these feelings faded with the release of the blood. It was as if they too gushed from my body onto that dirty, blood-spattered floor. My thoughts now pushing me further towards death and a longing for freedom. How long would freedom take to arrive? Had I cut deeply enough? Each cut taking me deeper away from myself.

One of the nurses burst into the room and, swearing, ran back out again. A dreadful commotion ensued with a doctor and several nurses carrying me out of the toilet, shouting over me, whilst attempting to stop the blood flow, as they waited for an ambulance to arrive.

"Leave me alone!" I mumbled, longing for oblivion to give me an escape out of there.

"Shut up and do as you're told," rasped Dr Webb, through gritted teeth.

At the general hospital I received emergency surgery, awakening the following day to find my arm in bandaging and foam padding, suspended from a frame above me. I had survived, again. Four days earlier I had taken a large overdose of paracetamol and had been told that I had been lucky to survive. Lucky?! I was *trying* to die. Surviving was not what I considered to be lucky. Surviving meant I got sent back to The Oak Unit under even stricter regimes than before.

The Oak Unit flashed through my mind. It was a place full of tears and screaming; so full, it felt like the walls would explode with the misery and angst they strained against, in an attempt to contain it for the people within who were unable to themselves. A secure communal membrane, a boundary that became shared between all the poor souls within who struggled with their own internal emotional membrane. Within the shared membrane, they were exposed to suffering on another level—they became one jigsaw piece amongst other pieces scattered all over the floor; each fighting to find their own picture, to hang on to themselves or to lose themselves. A community like no other hospital, somehow managing to swallow all sense of hope the moment you stepped across the threshold separating you from freedom and any sense of self that may have existed beforehand. And now I was going back.

When I awoke again I was in an empty cell, lying on the familiar red plastic mattress on the floor with my arm in a sling. Dr Lawton was sitting beside me, alone for a change, and with a look of unexpected concern, he said, "I am extremely worried about you at the moment, Beverley, and under no circumstances will you be allowed to leave this hospital. I am going to place you under a further Section. How do you feel about that?" What did I care anymore what they did to me? Despite the pain I was in, the desire to die was as strong as ever. Everybody knew that if I left the hospital I would immediately go back to starving. I replied, saying, "I don't know what's happening to me. I haven't got any control over my thoughts. Something else is controlling me and I feel like I am cracking up into a million pieces." He nodded, telling me that he was increasing my medication, before leaving me on my own again.

Dr Lawton's notes read:

> *'**24 June 1987:** Shortly after last interview yesterday afternoon, patient slashed her left forearm with a razor blade. She shows no evidence of clinical depression but her mental instability is such that she presents a real danger to herself. The nurses feel that they have no control over her as an informal patient.*
>
> *Detain Sec 3 if GP and Social Worker are in agreement.*
>
> *Beverley accepts that this is yet another refusal to accept responsibility for her actions but at the moment I can see no practical alternative.'*

That night my thoughts were intensely self-destructive: thoughts that took hold of me and were frantic and frightening. I was out of control, unable to fend off the onslaught. In sheer desperation, and to bring about an end to the raging turmoil in my head, I began to rip the stitches out of my arm with my teeth. I had no other means by which to mutilate myself and it felt as if I needed to tear myself apart to get at the thoughts. It was with utter frustration and hatred for the body that put me through such hell that I was driven to punish it.

I was interrupted by two male nurses who unlocked my cell door and, while one of them held me down on the plastic mattress on the floor, they injected me with a massive dose of Chlorpromazine (Largactil). They were laughing between themselves and, before leaving, they tied my hands together with the bandages I had removed from my arm in the hope of restraining me before the injection kicked in. They retreated from the cell, locking the door behind them. As I heard the door slam locked and heard their footsteps retreating down the corridor, I started biting through the bandages to release my hands. Within the supposedly safe space I was confined in, I now had the means to create a ligature. As soon as my hands were free, I tied the bandages around my neck and began to pull tight. The door burst open and the same two nurses barged in, removed the bandages from my neck and this time held me down until darkness swept over me. A mixed blessing.

Nursing Record reads:

> *'24 June 1987: Returned from RSCH with L forearm explored and sutured. Arm elevated and nursed in dressing gown. Will be seen by Dr Lawton—poss Sec 3 to be implemented.*
>
> *Nocte: Pt unable to settle down during the night—she is trying to kill herself by removing stitches to her arms. Duty Medical Officer informed about the behaviour and so PRN Largactil 100mg was prescribed and given about 12.30am by intramuscular injection. Obs maintained.'*

The following morning I was so full of drugs I could barely walk. I was routinely being given 100mg of Chlorpromazine before bed, and they had injected a further 100mg. I was also being given 50mg three times a day on top of this—but I was not psychotic! A nurse stayed behind to help me wash in a bathroom with no showers or baths, just a shared row of sinks that faced a row of polished metal sheets in place of mirrors. I was then helped downstairs through a sequence of doors, pausing to unlock and then lock each one, before we arrived in the secure day room. I slipped in and out of sleep, unaware of the time and vaguely disconnected from what was going on around me.

The Oak Unit 1987

Dr Marks, my GP, arrived mid-morning to see me at the request of Dr Lawton, a formality required for the new Section to be enforced. Since I had been Sectioned several times before by then, I was well accustomed to the procedure. It meant that I would be detained by law for a specific period of time, depending upon the Section chosen by those interviewing, usually at the suggestion of the consultant in charge. As Dr Marks had sent me to the hospital on a Section 2 (which lasted for 28 days), after my CPN had summoned his help after I'd overdosed, I could not be held under the same Section again. This meant I was facing a much lengthier Section since the next step up, a Section 3, lasted for six months. Different aspects of mental illness would need to justify the longer term involved and it also meant that treatment could be enforced. This was a serious situation to be in.

I was woken up and taken to the glass office, which provided the staff with visibility of the entire day room, entrance and corridors. It was with considerable planning and observation that I had managed to get past this unnoticed two days earlier when I had sneaked into the toilets to cut my wrist. With some surprise, I saw the familiar face of Dr Marks sitting at the desk inside. I tried to focus my eyes and my thoughts, fighting the drugs, in order to answer his questions, but I felt confused and humiliated. I was not allowed to wear my clothes and wore only a nightie, while everyone else was dressed normally, including the other patients. I was convinced that it would be obvious that I had gained weight through the force-feeding regimes, and this preoccupied me and caused me more shame than the predicament facing me.

One of the Charge-Nurses, Nigel, was trying to paint as black a picture as possible to Dr Marks. He was showing him my blood-test results from the paracetamol overdose, and with some animation was saying, "Just look at this! Look at her liver function results! She should have died from this!" As I sat there listening, I remembered another doctor at the hospital telling me that a person could die up to a fortnight after the overdose and not believing him. It was one thing to die when I planned it, but to die some time later when I was not expecting it was entirely different. Dr Marks smiled at me whilst waving Nigel to a seat at the back of the office, making it perfectly clear to him that he wanted to talk to me alone. "How have you been feeling since I last saw you?" he asked. "No different," I replied.

I wanted to tell him how life was sheer hell in The Oak Unit; how Nigel and another male Charge Nurse had threatened to lock me up, get me drunk and rape me in one of the cells upstairs while everyone else was downstairs. I wanted to tell him about the numerous occasions when other patients had threatened me, either sexually or physically, and how frightened I was. I wanted to tell him that they drugged me to the point that I couldn't walk—could barely move, in fact—and regularly had to face the indignity of being undressed by two nurses and locked in an empty cell. I wanted to tell him of the times when I had cried out from within the confines of that cell for my mum, for comfort, for anything, but nobody came. That if they did come, it was to laugh at me through the one-way mirror in the locked door, or to tell me to shut up, or to come bursting in, manhandling me down and restraining me whilst administering yet another injection. Whilst I couldn't see them on the other side of the door, I would be aware of hearing them on the other side of the one-way mirror in the door and could hear the voices and laughter on the other side. I wanted to tell him that I was surrounded by severely disturbed psychopathic patients, that I was usually the only female on the ward, the only one forced to stay in nightwear—and that it was sending me completely mad. In fact, there were no words with which to describe the way I was feeling since I had last seen him, so I remained silent. As silent as I'd always been. There had never been words for any of it.

Sitting there, feeling broken and totally alone, I listened while Dr Marks explained to me that he considered me to be an extremely high-risk patient at the moment and for that reason he was going to agree with Dr Lawton and sign the consent forms for a further Section. Still smiling, he said goodbye to me and I was shown out of the office. Two social workers arrived soon afterwards and, after speaking to me briefly, told me that they also agreed with the sectioning and would be signing their part of the papers accordingly. This was followed by a visit from two people representing the hospital management who came to read me my rights and to tell me that I would be detained on The Oak Unit for six months on a Section 3.

So, I faced six more months of hell, and then what? Would I ever be able to return to society? I doubted it. I could not imagine finding freedom after this. If I ever got out, I would return to starvation and die.

The Oak Unit 1987

In the meantime, if I got the opportunity, I would attempt to speed up the process. Death was the only way of attaining freedom, as ever.

My medication was increased further to the point at which I had neither the strength nor the will power to fight against it. Some days I ate, some I did not. Nobody cared. This was not a unit for treating anorexia, despite the pretense that they could. It was a secure unit; a prison for the mentally insane. It did not even employ normal nurses. The nurses here were predominantly male, on the large side and used to manhandling patients onto the floor and carrying them into cells to be restrained and injected into catatonic states of oblivion. Treatment consisted of drugs precipitated by violent outbursts, followed by more drugs. Maybe there was something symbolic in this for all of us of where we had come from: moments where the internal torment boiled over, pushing against the psychic membrane, seeking out oblivion and peace, which could only be achieved chemically after a messy struggle on the floor. How many of these troubled souls had entered the world in the same way, with a fight against leaving the safety of an internal warm membrane and into the harsh reality of a life of neglect or cruelty?

And so life went on in The Oak Unit. During the day I attempted to keep out of the way of the other patients as much as possible by curling up in a chair facing the wall. Night after night I suffered terrifying nightmares which seemed more real to me than my life on The Oak Unit. I was tormented by the feeling that an evil force seemed to be sucking me in towards it. I dreamt that the devil himself told me that he was in control of my life, and that he had my family in his grip too. I continued to keep my past to myself for fear that exposing the madness of it would prevent me from ever getting out.

Despite the size of the building, there were usually no more than seven patients at a time. These were severely disturbed people who were unable to be cared for within normal psychiatric units. Some were transferred for a day or two as a punishment for something they had done on another ward, or in another hospital, and the shock of time spent on The Oak Unit was usually enough to encourage co-operation when they were allowed to return. In the early days the same had happened to me, until the staff had simply given up and decided not to bother sending me back. My punishment was for taking laxatives, not because I was psychotic, although I had been addicted to over 135 laxatives a day before my admission and this caused serious concern over my potassium levels. I was told that the levels could fluctuate so rapidly that it would be impossible to prevent a heart attack if I tipped over a certain point. Equally, I was also using other methods for inducing vomiting which were so dangerous that there was a risk of liver damage, so whilst I wasn't psychotic, my illness was severe and unmanageable.

During my time at The Oak Unit, I met Lisa, a girl who was about my age (twenty-two), who had been in and out of there for several years. She wasn't there all the time, and I don't know where she went in between her stays. When she was admitted, she had allegedly been very slim and pretty, but by the time I met her, she appeared to have no idea of what was going on around her, of who she was, or what she looked like. She wore several layers of clothes, mostly inside out and back to front. Her hair was never brushed, was cut unevenly and stuck up all over her head. She tried to apply make-up to her face but would smear lipstick across her cheeks and her eyes were black smudges. Without warning, she would run from one side of the room to the other, screaming obscenities and attacking anyone in her path. Despite the similarity of age and gender, Lisa and I had nothing else in common and I never spoke to her during my time at The Oak Unit. She was an intimidating force to be reckoned with, as indeed were most of the male patients. Sometimes the unit would allow Lisa to go out for a walk only to receive a frantic phone call saying that she had molested a man in the nearby village, and would somebody come and get her. My greatest fear was that if they made me stay, I would end up like Lisa.

Then there was Ed. Ed looked to be in his 60s and had been living as a tramp before coming to The Oak Unit. He had no clothes or belongings and so he wore a pair of dingy grey hospital pyjamas. It soon became apparent that he was more accustomed to being without clothes because he seemed unable to keep them on. He would roll around on the floor moaning and groaning and then would charge, quite suddenly, from one end of the room to the other, yelling, as Lisa did. He was a very tall, completely bald man, with sore-looking skin that constantly oozed blood. He too seemed unaware of either his surroundings or other people and would even relieve himself in the plant pots in the day room. He was another whom I tried to avoid at all cost.

Much of the time I kept my eyes shut, being completely consumed by my own internal thought processes and battle. Sometimes I would watch what was going on around me for fear of getting caught up in it, but usually the others sat in a different room to the one I chose, because there they could smoke. They had a television in the smoking room, housed in an enormous cabinet with a scratched and nicotine-stained Perspex front to it. Although essential to protect it from the frequent violent outbursts, the panel made it impossible to see the television screen properly but, since the audience were so heavily sedated, it probably made little difference. The television remained switched on for the majority of the time, pointlessly beaming out through the thick smog of the smoking room.

One morning I was summoned by my consultant Dr Lawton to meet with him and one of his colleagues. The discussion went from bad to worse. Dr Lawton asked several questions about events leading up to my admission while the other doctor took notes, and then he began to get very angry with me. "You are behaving like a spoilt five-year-old! You refused to cooperate with the treatment on Forrest Ward earlier this year, and now you are doing exactly the same thing here on The Oak Unit!" This made me livid and I began to shout back at him. Again, he asked me, "Why did you take the overdose?" I replied, "Because I am sick and tired of being the way I am! Sick of all the laxatives, sick of my obsession with my weight and food." In exasperation he said, "It is all within your power to stop, but you are just too bloody minded. I'm as sick of it as you are!"

"I know you are!" I screamed back at him.

Dr Lawton's notes read:

> *'Attitude remains essentially unchanged—attention seeking, self-pitying and, in essence, demanding a magical situation where is eating and not eating at the same time. Still talks of being possessed by and controlled by her 'obsession' and protests that she cannot help herself.'*

I just did not seem to be able to get through to any of them. I was completely frustrated by their inability to comprehend what I was going through. Everyone, including the doctors, assumed that I could simply snap out of the anorexia back to normality, but it was impossible. The more they tried to force me to eat, the more I rebelled—not to be difficult, but because they were not dealing with the underlying issues and I was not able to eat while they remained. (Not that I knew what they were, because as long as I remained anorectic, my problems were concealed beneath and I had now completely lost touch with them.) The more the doctors and nurses got cross and fed up, the more hopeless I felt.

"I don't know why I feel like this. I wish you would do something to stop these thoughts. My mind is totally preoccupied with these obsessions and the overwhelming urge for self-destruction that I can't stand anymore of it."

The tone of Dr Lawton's voice softened, "If you don't start eating again, you're going to die."

"That's the general idea!" I screamed.

Chapter 3

The Presenting Past 2004

THESE WERE NOT MY THOUGHTS and I appealed to this new person who called herself 'Nothing.' Nothing appeared to be older than Evie, a fourteen year old alter, associated with anorexia. "Nothing," I said, "You have been stuck there for the past 20 years, when everything and everyone around you has moved on. It doesn't have to be like this—you can be free. You can choose to live. It may not feel like it now, but you can choose."

But as she whipped around to face me in my mind, her face contorted with disgust, she snapped angrily, "No! You don't understand. This is my life. I'm anorexic—that's who I am. There's nothing else anymore. No hope. No chance of recovery or change. I need to lose weight—that's all that matters. Everything else has gone." So, I discovered Nothing was an anorectic part of me.

"That's not true," I pleaded with her. "You have a name and you are loved. You are not 'Nothing,' nor are you 'Anorexic,' despite what it looks and feels like now. You are 'Cherished.' Look how much He cares for you and holds out His hand to you. Reach out, take it, and see for yourself. Trust me with this because we've already overcome this once. He chose you before the creation of the world. You have been adopted as His child and marked with His seal. He knit you together in your mother's womb. You have been fearfully and wonderfully made."

Nothing drifted away, unable to retain any of these words, her intrusion into my world momentarily suspended. Despite the fact that I knew my identity as a child of God, and had helped others to renew their own minds with the truth, these other parts buried within my own mind, over which I had no control, did not know that they were precious, loved children of God. Here, in this paradox hidden within my own unconscious mind, was an experience representative of something of the split between good and bad that had caused me significant distress since early childhood. My own mind would have been switching backward and forward between trying to live a normal life whilst carrying the burden of untold fear and horror. The childhood nightmares of revolving images, roundabouts circling faster and faster, switching between good and evil. Not only was my mind trying to process how parents could be both good and bad, but equally fighting to process the internal conflict between normal childhood experiences and the ones it was hiding from me.

It was going to be a long ride before this carousel stopped spinning and would let the children off. Nothing had a piece of me, as did Evie, and several others, and they needed to taste freedom and discover the truth for themselves, but they just weren't getting it. How could this be true? It was one thing trying to convince other people to trust God with their pain and let go of their pasts, but how did you go about convincing a part of your own mind when you thought that you were already convinced? How could another part of you not know it when the rest of me knew it so completely? I knew that if I could grasp this, then I would grasp it for others stuck in the same quandary and this became my prayer. I didn't know the answers, but I knew that God did.

My heart broke for all of them, but I was also frustrated and annoyed with them too, as I couldn't understand what was going on. I longed to reach out to them and make whatever it was go away, to tell them it didn't matter anymore whatever anybody had done or said because they were so loved and special and it was all in the past. But they refused to hear, it seemed, confusing as that was—how could they refuse to hear when I chose to?

> *"I can't. I'm too afraid of gaining weight. I'll lose control. I can't trust anybody. I want to lose more weight, more than anything else in the world. Please help me,"* wrote Nothing in my journal.

And Nothing had achieved simply that. She could slip in and out of me as and when she chose. "Hear what He says to you, Nothing," I said to her within my mind,

> *I have loved you with an everlasting love; I have drawn you with loving kindness. I will build you up again and you will be rebuilt. You will take up your tambourine and go out to dance with the joyful again. Jeremiah 31:3–4*

It seemed like total madness trying to convince a part of myself of something I already believed with all my heart. But, amazing as it seemed, this part of me hadn't heard these words before. Then there before me, like an apparition, Nothing appeared; her arms hanging loosely by her side, her empty dead eyes staring out, fear long gone, or else she was just resigned to it.

"Nothing, can you trust me?" I whispered. "Can you allow me to know who and what did this to you so I can help you? Nothing, can you hear me?" It felt like I was trying to trick her into telling me some terrible secret but surely it was my secret as well, wasn't it? She was keeping it from me and it was my life, not hers, that was being messed up by this. After all, she wasn't real. Or was it me that wasn't real? It was hard to know at times.

And then I felt 'Bad' for the first time, her voice soft within my heart, very different to Nothing or Evie.

"I'm bad. Very, very bad."

In my head I found myself responding. "That's not true. How can you be so bad?" I searched right back, trying to retrieve any memories I'd laid aside for what could possibly be so bad. I searched as far back as I could but I couldn't recall anything that made me that bad. Then I heard her speak again. My heart was racing now; my head searching for answers. Surely, I'd remember something as wicked as this feeling. . .but, oh Lord, I could feel it deep inside me: such overwhelming pain and guilt. Tears flowing down her cheeks, the stifled screams, the agony written all over her face. I could see people. She's being held there, forced to look.

"It's not daddy's fault. He didn't know this was going to happen. This is a terrible mistake! It's not daddy's fault. It's not his fault. . ."

Her little voice was going round and round in my head as I allowed myself to feel her thoughts and see her memories, and it all fell into place. "Yes, they hurt you terribly," I said, "but that doesn't make you bad. You were too little to be responsible for any of this. It wasn't your fault. You can let go of this now. It's over. Listen, see He speaks to you as well."

> *Do not be afraid of them, for I am with you and will rescue you. Jeremiah 1:8*

I was determined to conceal to the outside world how my inner world was crumbling, how it had long since disintegrated. Up until then, nobody would have known the pain and the memories that I was fighting but which were now spilling out everywhere. My default position if I got overwhelmed had always been to stop eating, or to stop living altogether on a conscious level: to dissociate.

I decided to try psychotherapy. I sat in the chair opposite Richard, unable to make eye contact and unable to express why I was there or what had brought me to this point. Evie would take over the moment I walked through the door of the clinic, desperate to tell her story and ask for help, but then unable to find a voice. She seemed lost, frightened, and greatly troubled, as I was as equally confused by her emergence, which seemed to come out of nowhere.

Sometimes the parts were angry and I found myself accusing Richard of not listening, of getting it wrong, not smiling the way they wanted him to. Other times the dependency upon him was hard to bear, but he remained constant and listened to what was brought so we could gradually bring it together over time. As we did, my mind's attempts to repress material became ever more desperate.

The key for Richard was in providing a safe place to come to, to demonstrate that he was able to tolerate whatever was said without judgment, to be with me in whatever situation I was in at the time. I longed for him to be able to relate to the parts, whilst, at the same time, battled with the need to hide them.

> *"There are times when my head feels so spongy, like weird thoughts are being stretched like chewing gum and colours flash through like stained-glass windows. When you feel like you must be high, like you could do everything, or collapse incapable of anything. I'm tired of fighting this. Have I survived, and at what cost? I want to feel safe and to be loved. I want my dad to be normal and to love me. I wish you loved me, dad. No. There are times when pretending to be strong is as good as it gets, and my head feels like a bubble gum bubble about to burst. . ."*

> *"The feelings are building up again and I am connecting with the strange 'compulsion to run away' part of me as I can't cope at all with being fat. I hate my body—I am disgusting. I mustn't say that because God created me, so I am fearfully and wonderfully made, but I've messed it up. I'm disgusting. I'm sorry, God. I'm hurting and getting desperate with this situation. I am simply tired of living like this."*

> *". . .Nobody ever comes, nobody takes it away."*

Until Evie or any of the others were willing to integrate and fuse with me, I had to stand in that gap and claim the truth for them. I could speak over them that I had not been given a spirit of fear, but of power, love and a sound mind (2Timothy 1:7 NKJV) and claim it for every part of me as I tried to teach them, as I had my own children, how to believe in the power of God's word.

I responded to these thoughts as I always did. "You can choose whether to listen to these thoughts or dismiss them as lies from the enemy. They are not your thoughts and you have the authority to make them stop."

"I don't want to go down again. I need a sticking plaster to put over it right now. I want to get off this merry-go-round," one part argued.

"Evie," I said (not knowing which part I was actually addressing most of the time), "you don't need a sticking plaster; in fact, the very opposite, because you need to allow this all to come out in order for God to pour in His healing love. He will protect you and lead you by the hand along this journey of recovery."

Despite the fact that I had been free of anorexia for a number of years prior to this, starving was the method I knew for controlling distress. This meant therapy was delayed for a while until I was ready to move on again. Richard didn't show any special interest in the behaviour patterns I was exhibiting, but continued to show he cared by being there and providing a safe place where I knew that I was heard. The starving of course, made the depression worse, which in turn made the dissociating worse. The thoughts and behaviour became more and more unmanageable as Nothing took over and projected all her anger into food and starving.

It was as if as Evie and the others allowed aspects of themselves to be seen, the intense feelings each carried also came gushing forth with them. I hoped that eventually we would get to know what was beneath it all, but I had to wait for the truth to surface in God's time, if it ever did. In the meantime, I had to trust in God's perfect timing and rest in the safe knowledge that it was in His control. I didn't doubt that if Evie and the others developed their own faith and understanding of renewing their own mind with the truth, as I had done, that they would one day conquer all that was tormenting them and that kept them prisoner, and this would then allow them to fuse with the rest of me.

Chapter 4

The Blue Room 1971

WITH THE WIND RUSHING past my face and my hair flying out behind me, momentarily everything seemed strangely familiar again. Deep in thought, I let the swing come slowly to a standstill. As I looked down at the buttons on my knitted blue dress, I was aware of a sense of déjà vu which, whilst it intrigued me, was also unnerving. Sometimes it felt as if I was living in a dream, like nothing was real anymore. I sensed an emptiness and an aching inside myself for something that wasn't there, along with a desperate sense of unease. I was only seven and I didn't understand what any of this meant. I hopped off the swing to wander down the path at the side of the house, with no particular objective in mind. Orange-blossom overhanging the path filled the air with its sweet, heady aroma. Always being in the shade and home to the dustbin meant the path was dank with other more unpleasant smells at times.

It immediately took my mind back to the recurring nightmares I suffered: a never-ending cycle of revolving images and sensations that switched from light to dark. A carousel, spinning faster and faster, with the scene switching from delicate white daisies to foreboding leather, although I had no understanding of why the leather felt so dangerous. There was something about the switching images that made me feel physically sick. It was a familiar conflict that made no sense at the time: a battle between good and evil, that would make a habit of repeating throughout my life.

Later that night as I lay precariously close to slipping and giving myself away, I peered through the banisters to catch a glimpse of the group of people gathering in the room below. Nervously, I tried to catch an odd word that would give me some indication as to what was going on. Some of the faces I recognised, but others were strangers. A black-bearded man, with piercing eyes, made me feel particularly uneasy. There was something strangely sinister about him and, as his eyes caught mine and held them, I froze. They met every Monday evening throughout my childhood, and I knew that I didn't like what they were doing.

As I returned to my bed, troubled and restless, my thoughts turned as usual to my younger sister, Louisa. Anger and jealousy surfaced as I wondered how it was possible that she could be so apparently happy when I wasn't. I felt different. Unloved. I felt as if I had to carefully hide how I really felt, as if my life depended on it—if they knew the fear and pain inside me, then I would be loved less: as if the pain was somehow proof of badness. Louisa, with her dark blonde hair, petite, and elfin-like features, against me who was dark and well built. Another of those contrasts that troubled me so greatly, and how my immature mind attempted to make sense of the physical difference that must be the explanation for why I was the one they couldn't love.

As I looked down at myself, at the tree-trunk legs I hated, as I perceived them, I was consumed with jealousy and hatred for my sister. Deep inside me, I knew my hatred was toxic and vile.

Perhaps hating Louisa was easier than allowing myself to be frightened by them because I needed to depend on them and keep them good. Hating her would soon be turned completely in on myself, and I became the hateful object. Every waking, breathing moment, I was scared of what mum and dad were doing, but I was even more scared of telling them because I knew how important it was to them. But what exactly were they doing?

I grew up with a sense of what my life had been about, only to discover years later that I knew nothing of the truth. I discovered that amongst the fear, seeds were being sown that were meant to be remembered to throw me off course. These fragments of stories were terrifying, and forced me into a life of silence or to risk ridicule. Behind the stories, was another story far more shocking and harder to believe than the one that I was permitted to fear.

For now, we will follow what I thought happened, or *appeared* to happen. A half-story, a fragmented half-life, which made no sense, and wouldn't do for years to come.

And so it was that I found myself, now aged ten, and wandering up and down the aisles of trestle tables at the local jumble sale when I came across something that caught my eye. Mum and dad were on the other side of the hall when I picked up the simple pewter crucifix. Momentarily mesmerised by the cross and holding on to it tightly, I felt a sense of peace and safety wash over me. A quick search of my pockets produced enough change for it to become mine and, as I tucked it away discreetly and carefully into my pocket, I scanned the hall across a sea of preoccupied people for the others.

I don't know why it caught my eye, or why I thought it would save me from my fear, but I took that cross home with me in confidence. Every night I lay staring at it, mesmerised, trying to block out the fear, and praying the Lord's Prayer over and over until sleep would eventually get the better of me. Often, I would hold it, as I first had done in the village hall, for comfort and safety when I had nowhere else to run.

Alone in my bedroom one weekend, that familiar fear began creeping up on me again, hanging in the air. A fear that was becoming increasingly well-known to me by then, but I nevertheless didn't understand. I turned and saw the cross out of the corner of my eye, Jesus hanging there, glinting in the sun on my windowsill. Transfixed, I walked over and lifted it down, hugging it to myself for reassurance and protection. As it rested gently in my palm it felt warm and safe. It grew warmer. Hotter. The terror didn't set in immediately because my mind refused to accept what was happening. Staring down at it in absolute disbelief, I watched as the cross began to bend double in my hands, whilst burning me with intense heat. Time seemed to stand still as I was drawn into what was occurring before my eyes. As if suddenly brought back to my senses, I dropped the cross to the floor as terror, shock, and pain hit me all at once. I tore down the six flights of stairs from my attic room, round and round, slipping and stumbling over several steps at a time, screaming as I went, until I landed in the hallway in a state of unimaginable fright, like a tangled bag of squirrels. There I sat, stunned, huddled in a heap at the bottom of the stairs, unable to look behind me in trepidation of what might have followed me down from the attic.

Every part of my being felt repulsion and disgust for what I had just witnessed through something that in my mind was supposed to protect me. There was that same familiar conflict, raising its ugly head again: good and evil together. Shame and embarrassment rapidly set in with the realisation that I was revealing something of the fear I fought so hard to suppress and conceal from them.

Deep inside me my heart was crying out, "Mummy, help me! Please make it stop!" But nothing seemed to frighten them, and to make it worse, they found it funny and seemed to be laughing at me. There was nobody to turn to with this ever-growing fear developing inside me like a malignant cancer. I wasn't allowed to tell anybody anything because "other people won't understand," they said, and yet it somehow seemed as if it was an honour to be let in on this secret—a secret about the reality of the supernatural realm we lived in. This was apparently normal, but I had no way of questioning it. I didn't know any different, but I didn't understand why I couldn't cope with what was supposed to be 'normal'.

If it was wrong to be afraid then I couldn't ever own up to it, but I was drowning in fear.

I sat rocking on the stairs, frightened and thinking, "I'll run away. When I'm sixteen I'll be big enough to go." Backwards and forwards, rocking, rocking, getting increasingly more unsettled by the persistent fear as time went by because I still didn't actually know what it was that was so wrong.

I've got to run away. This was a theme that stuck with me all my life. Random insignificant events that would trigger the same thought process and I would be struck with the overwhelming desire to run as an adult—but run from what? I didn't know then, nor did I for years to come. Instead, I ran away in my mind, shutting everything down, hiding it away, burying it. I didn't do that on my own, for I was being trained to forget.

Fernhill was an imposing white house perched on the edge of hills overlooking the valley below, with views for miles. There were seven bedrooms and two staircases, which would have been great fun for games of hide-and-seek, but there wasn't much playing going on in that house. We moved to Fernhill in the summer holidays of 1977 and come September, I was starting at secondary school across town. I was one of a minority who wanted to learn and so it didn't do me any favours in the popularity stakes. By the end of the year, however, I had become increasingly more depressed and unpopular. I was being teased for working hard, teased for being fat until finally, having had enough of the name-calling and lack of fun in my life, I resolved to change. What followed, at age of thirteen now, was the first of a complete change of personality, a switch, that wouldn't make sense until years later.

Meanwhile, it wasn't just at school where things were becoming increasingly more intolerable. Life at home was becoming extremely bizarre. The group of people who came to the house every week continued after the move to Fernhill, seemingly taking on a new stance with the arrival of another member to the group. Ivy was a rather strange elderly woman, who mum and dad told us was an alien from Venus (she may not have looked strange, of course, but as we were led to believe she was an alien, she was strange, whatever she actually looked like). This was perhaps the beginnings of many stories as things were being ramped up. This, I was meant to remember. Previously the group met to 'meditate' and communicate with spirits in the blue room, but now they were allegedly communicating with 'superior beings from outer space.' Ivy loaned mum and dad a telescope with which to keep an eye on the sky at night for flying saucers.

"Wake up! Wake up, quickly!" came mum's voice late one night.

"Why?" I mumbled sleepily, immediately feeling a sense of impending doom.

"A flying saucer is landing tonight. Get up now!"

Louisa and I were bundled out of bed and into the car in a rush, still in our nighties, with not a moment to argue. As dad drove, mum explained that a flying saucer was landing at Newlands Corner in Surrey that night and we were going to leave with them in the saucer. As I fumbled for the door lock in terror, mum laughed, announcing that I need not bother because aliens had telekinetic powers that could unlock car doors. I sat there, frozen to my seat, paralyzed with fear. For the rest of the drive, Louisa and I sat in silence, until we reached the public car park at Newlands Corner in the middle of the night. We sat on the edge of a precipice for longer than I care to remember, staring out across the pitch-black landscape. Waiting. I have no memory of getting back home again that night, or whether we met anybody or not, but it would later become apparent that this was an event that could never be spoken of. The reasons for which became clearer later—if we told anybody, then nobody would ever believe anything else we said.

During this period, mum was taking lessons to develop her psychic powers. One of the tools she invested in was a crystal ball, purchased from the annual Body, Mind, and Spirit exhibition in London that they took us to. Every now and again she would take herself off to her bedroom to practice, leaving instructions not to be disturbed. It was on one such occasion when Louisa and I were playing downstairs when we heard a long protracted scream from upstairs, barely recognisable as mum. As we ran for the stairs, dad brushed us both aside, yelling brusquely, "Stay there!" as he bounded up, two or three steps at a time, towards the scream. Glued to the spot, we stayed right there at the bottom of the stairs, waiting. The crystal ball had become so boiling hot that her hands had stuck to its surface as it continued to burn her flesh. I don't know how dad freed her hands, but the ball was put back into its packaging and confined amongst the jumpers in mum's wardrobe.

After this event Louisa made the sudden and understandable announcement that she didn't believe in God anymore, altogether denying the existence of a spiritual world. She never budged from this viewpoint again. I knew exactly how she felt and even admired her for it to some degree at the time, but I had found a refuge in God and wasn't going to let go of Him.

For me, however, there was no denying it: there were spirits everywhere, surrounding me all the time—when I used the loo, had a bath, and especially when I shut my eyes to sleep. Then, I would be vulnerable and unable to defend myself should they come for me in the night. How did I suppose they would come for me and what would they do to me if they did? I didn't know, but I hugged my knees to my chest as usual, praying, and trying to make myself as small as possible, trying to stay awake.

The room was in semi-darkness when I went in. A foreboding heaviness lingered in the air. I felt a strange sense of disquiet, mixed with inquisitiveness. I was fourteen now and had been asking endless questions about the goings-on in the blue room, needing to feel included in whatever it was that was so important, so precious to them. Every Monday Louisa and I had to stay in our rooms, knowing instinctively to be quiet. We didn't even talk to each other but remained in isolation in our own bedrooms. Or so I thought. What I knew was that there was something mysterious and terrifying about the blue room, something that frightened us so much that we weren't even able to confide in each other for making it more real. But, none of it was real, it was all a game. A complicated, nasty game. Hanging on the wall of the blue room was a beautiful painting of Jesus surrounded by children and sheep, with the words underneath, 'Loving Shepherd of thy sheep.' Why my dad bought it and hung it there when he didn't believe in Jesus, I never knew. I loved that painting, and it's mine now, one of the only things I have from my childhood.

'Christos,' as they referred to it, was a regression technique through which they believed that you relived past lives. The group had been experimenting with Christos for some time by then and it was my turn. As I lay down on the settee surrounded by the group of adults, one of them clenched her hand into a fist and began rubbing my forehead in a circular motion as she explained that this was the position of the 'third eye.' Another massaged my feet in the same circular motion. Both points were believed, by them, to be the exit points for the soul. Looking up towards the ceiling I became aware of three shadowy black beings staring back down at me.

Dad was to be my point of reference between the physical and spiritual world. He would guide me by asking questions and I was to report back everything to him as it happened. Therefore it was dad who suggested to me that it was time to leave my body and to move towards those dark beings. As I allowed my mind to follow his words I became aware of being able to look down on my body from the ceiling as if it was somebody else lying there, after which the sky seemed to open up before me and I was flying. The land spread out below as if I was in an invisible helicopter surrounded by bright blue sky. I would have been happy to continue flying but dad was directing me to land.

As I started the descent, I was aware of a mass of quizzical black faces below staring up at me. Flying through the air had felt entirely natural but the surprised expressions below made me uneasy. I landed amongst the huge crowd whilst dad was asking me to tell him who I was. It felt awkward at first talking to him whilst surrounded by this unknown crowd but as I looked down at myself the rest of my surroundings faded and I saw that I was now wearing a long gown and was able to report back that my name was Mary.

"What's happening? Where are you?" dad questioned before asking me to move on in time. I was standing by a quayside looking out across the sea and was crying bitterly. "Why are you crying?" dad was enquiring in a subdued monotone

"He's leaving me!" I sobbed.

I couldn't stop crying, couldn't rid myself of intense grief, my own disconnected grief for something that I couldn't see, despite the fact that dad was trying to direct me to move on in time. When I remained caught up in that moment they brought the session to a close but the room remained in semi-darkness and the group continued in meditation. What grief had I connected to? Was it mine, or Mary's? Who was Mary?

Nobody communicated; the room was silent. Almost immediately after I closed my eyes again, a leather-clad hand reached from behind and grabbed me around my mouth, yanking my head back. With sheer terror I saw the guillotine above me moments before it dropped and, in one fell swoop, severed my legs from the remainder of my body. Letting out an almighty scream I couldn't hold back… and the guillotine faded as if never there and the group turned to stare at me as I looked down at my legs to see that they were still attached. What had just happened? Had I tapped into something within my unconscious in that moment through their meddling? What did it mean? Had I remembered something I was meant to forget?

None of it made any sense, but as we drove home that night, I felt disconnected and traumatised. I watched the world pass by on the other side of the car window as if I were half-heartedly aware of a silent movie playing out on the other side of the glass. The world was passing me by and I was unable to tell anybody how mine was making me feel. As I lay on my bed that night, unable to sleep for thinking about the earlier events of that evening, I tried to focus my eyes on familiar objects in my room. I realized that I couldn't see them properly because obscuring my view was what appeared to be another transparent world overlapping mine, with walls, angles, and corners that didn't belong there. I became increasingly alarmed as I began to feel I wasn't a part of anything real anymore. I seemed to be slipping between two dimensions, unable to tell what was real and what wasn't: a co-conscious dissociative episode of derealisation and depersonalisation.

I heard a voice scream from within the silence. "Dad!" It was me screaming, trying to muster all the energy I could to find a voice in this strange void within my bedroom. A voice from somewhere, somebody, from within my own mind, but strangely separate from me.

Dad drew a circle of salt around me on the bed, instructing me to perform 'exercises' that were supposed to draw my soul back into my body, explaining that my soul had been left half in my body and half out. Eventually I drifted off into a fitful sleep. I had nearly lost my soul apparently, but maybe I had, instead, created a new one that I had just caught a glimpse of. There were probably several others by this time as well, but I was about to make another major switch and let another part of me take over. I may not have been a Monarch butterfly yet, but a metamorphic transition was taking place.

In that moment I had experienced a glimpse of what my life would look like in years to come. It would be many years later when a significant traumatic experience would show me how I had developed a window within my mind that I could slip through when I felt overwhelmed by fear or pain. It was not that my soul had been 'left half in and half out of my body,' although in some respects that sums up the way it felt at times, but that my personality had been shattered by fear. As each shard slipped in and out of having conscious control, there would, at times, be an experience of co-conscious awareness of the experience—as there had been that night—whilst at other times I was protected from knowing reality. Each fragmented alter personality became adept at carrying the secret to protect me from knowing the full horror of my life.

This is not something that develops in teenage life but is something that develops as a way of coping with extreme trauma or fear usually before the age of five, therefore suggesting that this episode had not been the first time. Dissociative Identity Disorder (DID), formerly known as multiple personality disorder, is a creative and adaptive attempt by the brain to manage extreme trauma which enables a child to survive and carry on living, alongside horrific experiences that he or she can't escape from. The brain manages to block the trauma from awareness by forcing it into other personalities. The child lives a dual—or multiple—life, protected from knowing what is happening in one part of their life so that they can go to school and take part in normal activities. When they are faced with what they cannot cope with, they switch into the personality (or part) that the mind has created to take it for them. When it is over, this part switches back out and either other parts switch in to carry the aftermath, or the host personality switches back in, without awareness of what has just taken place. The parts form 'a system' that work together to protect the host from knowing; although this is just a simplified explanation of something in fact very complex.

Whilst I had no awareness of the way I was living and experiencing life, I was aware that I wasn't happy and that it had always been this way. Inside I knew that I was falling apart, and felt as if I was fighting to keep up the pretence of putting on an act of doing well. I had no idea how I was falling apart or how hard the other parts of myself were fighting to hide it. The internal battle I felt from fighting to keep up an act was an accurate description, but it wasn't the pressure of putting on an act for my parents, as I thought, but was in fact the pressure of hiding reality from myself, caused by the enormous tension generated by slipping between levels of conscious awareness and amnesia.

I wanted their love so badly. I had been about ten years old when I told dad that I was going to commit suicide when I grew up. "I have this strange feeling inside me that I'm going to be a drug addict when I grow up and I'm going to die of an overdose!" I told him, nonchalantly, one day. I felt it as if it were a curse over my life and I was stating fact; but it was received without concern and laughed off. Surely any parent would be alarmed by a statement like this from their ten-year-old daughter, whilst instead it was dismissed. But where had the thought come from? If everything was 'normal,' from where did it stem and why weren't they alarmed? Why the need to run from a normal, relatively privileged family life, albeit with some weird spiritual beliefs which we weren't allowed to talk about?

Chapter 5

Hungry 1979

INGRAINED WITHIN THE WEB that was being finely spun within my mind, was the instruction to never tell a soul. Perhaps something of the fear of the consequences of what would happen if I did had risen to conscious recall, without connection to anything else. I later suspected that it was sown into the whole system so the threat of ever saying anything would filter through to a conscious level.

I was aware of collapsing with some regularity during periods at home. Intense pain would cause me to fall to the floor and render me completely unable to move. I was not aware of why I fell, and no doctor or ambulance was ever called, no visit to the GP surgery, no questioning, just what appeared to be an acceptance that this happened. It never happened at school, only when dad was home. He would pick me up and carry me upstairs to their bed. I was given a crushed tablet mixed with Ribena on a spoon and read a story—not a children's story as you would imagine when a child is sick and in pain, but a strange book from dad's bedside table. I would then sleep. Reality was maybe different in that I was being led on a journey of dissociation, with a tale that encouraged further disintegration and lead me further away from everything real. Traps were being laid like bombs within my mind, as I was led down rabbit warrens and tunnels, further and further away, on a course set to control and create compliance.

But things didn't go to plan and a new plan had to be set in motion. The new plan led to another shift that took place, and the creation of a new part—'Nothing'.

It was April 1979 when Mum told me that her marriage to dad had been a mistake—she was meant to be with someone else, a man who worked for my dad. She told me that they had been married to each other in several previous lives and were meant to be together again! Her dead father, who'd been killed in the second world war, told her this, she said.

The news was so shocking because it felt as if 'the spirit world' had finally won. It felt as if everything I had been fighting against for the previous fourteen years had been for nothing. I didn't understand it then, but this was to be my way out, my escape from the role ahead for me. But I was a mess, by deliberate design, and this wasn't part of the plan.

It was, however, part of God's plan, because by then, I had been praying for years to be rescued. Now He was reaching in to pull me out, although I didn't see it like that at the time as everything felt extremely traumatic.

I blamed myself, as every child usually does for her parents' failed marriage. "If they loved me more, then this wouldn't be happening," is the unconscious reasoning of every child because every child believes she is the centre of everything even when she's the centre of something else, as I was. With this news adding to the helplessness I already felt, I lost my appetite and a deeper sense of depression set in. I went from top of my class to practically bottom. Weight fell off rapidly and I quickly developed an obsession with weight loss and starvation that became a successful distraction from the fear and desperate unhappiness I felt inside.

It was about this time that mum and dad told me that they and the rest of their group members were the reincarnations of the disciples. Mum was apparently Peter and dad was Luke, another friend of theirs who ran a local sweet shop was John the Baptist. They believed they communicated with another disciple, Andrew, in the blue room. It felt even more wrong to be afraid if they were who they said they were, as surely they had to be good. This was another one of the seeds being sown that I was meant to remember. Who would ever tell anybody, especially the doctors treating your anorexia, that your parents were the reincarnations of the disciples? It served to create more internal chaos and devotion to their cause.

There were lots of arguments going on between them both, and lots of crying. Inside I was crying too, believing that nobody loved me or cared. This was true, in fact: they didn't. I wrote in a diary every day, where I poured out my heartache and yearning for love, along with a desperation to never feel again. And I prayed.

"Our Father who art in heaven, hallowed be thy name..." I'm so frightened, I can't shut my eyes. I can't turn the light off because then I won't be able to see. But I can't see *them* with the light on either, even though I know they're here. I'm so tired, but I can't sleep because if I lose control, then *they* might get me. I can't put my legs out straight because then my feet will be too near the end of the bed and I can't see what's at the end of the bed. *They* might pull me out by my feet. I have to keep as small as I can be.

"Thy kingdom come, thy will be done, on earth as it is in heaven..." I'm so frightened. Jesus, please help me.

"Give us this day our daily bread..." Please help me to starve and lose more weight.

"And forgive us our trespasses as we forgive those who trespass against us. Lead us not into temptation and deliver us from evil..." Please don't let them get me, Lord. Please make them go away.

"For thine is the kingdom, the power, and the glory, forever and ever, Amen. Our Father who art in heaven, hallowed be thy name..." Dear Lord God, I'm so frightened. Please help me. Please help me...

Every night the same routine: sheer terror, curled up in a ball, repeating the Lord's Prayer over and over until I couldn't keep my eyes open any longer.

A visitor was coming to see me, they said. A 'hypnotist' who would hypnotise me to eat and get better from anorexia. I didn't want to get better. I wanted to lose more weight. I didn't understand the significance of the visit at the time, but it seemed odd that he would come so late in the evening while their weekly group was meeting. He was travelling a long way to see me, I was told, which was why he was coming so late in the evening. I was instructed to give him some dinner when he arrived, while they were in the blue room, and he would talk to me on my own. Afterwards he told me that he wasn't going to hypnotise me to get better, and he seemed to take some delight in saying this. Surely, he hadn't come all this way to tell me this, although I was very relieved not to be hypnotised to make me eat. This was a bizarre meeting that didn't make any sense at all, but not much in life did.

I think I *was* 'hypnotised' that night, but not to make me eat, but because information had to be erased. I suspect that the group were involved in using a form of mind-control, whether knowingly or unknowingly, with links to others. I am sure that my dad knew what he was doing and I don't believe he acted alone. The group was being disbanded and I no longer served a purpose to him.

But God had other plans. This was not the end for me, even though it looked like it.

God was there, but He seemed to be standing to one side, leaving me to fight this battle on my own. I lay in the bath, feeling miserable and very lonely. Life was so confusing and I was isolated and shut off from reality, becoming more and more distant from friends at school. The faint watery light from the sun just managed to glint off the bubbles of distorted glass in the bathroom window. Staring at it, I found myself praying and asking Jesus to come into my life. I had been attending confirmation classes and, although this may seem like an odd thing to have done in the circumstances, dad had always spoken about Jesus to me, and I had been turning to Jesus myself for several years. Dad had his own views as to who Jesus was and I think this was all part of the conspiracy and confusion. But whatever they were up to, I did find God.

As I gazed at the faint sunlight glistening on the bathroom window, a ball of light seemed to come through the glass. Increasing in brightness and size as I stared at it, mesmerised in wonder, the light began to descend until I found myself immersed in luminous golden rays. As if everything was happening in slow motion, two hands materialised out of the glowing brilliance. Momentarily suspended within the light, the hands then came to rest on each of my own hands before disappearing through my skin. His arms were reaching down inside my own, as if mine were merely the sleeves, and His fingers filling my own as if I were the gloves. I lay in the warm water, filled in that moment with His Holy Spirit, washing through me with an inner warmth of His love.

I felt completely at peace and at no moment the least bit afraid, despite all the previous occult experiences. I knew deep within me that I was experiencing God's love and I knew that the hands belonged to Jesus. My whole body was washed through with His pure water; perfect love and peace filling every part of me. I lay there soaking in the warmth of His golden light, breathing in the sheer beauty and holding it secretly within my heart.

My love for Jesus became as overwhelming as, in that moment, I had been made aware of His love for me too. It outweighed any emotional feelings I had ever known. I needed to know He was there and I wasn't alone. He was with me for the next part of His elaborate and dangerous escape plan. It wasn't going to be easy, and there was a long struggle ahead to disentangle myself from the web that had been created in my mind. But God is the Creator of all things, and He was drawing me back to Himself, reconnecting me to Him, slowly and carefully unravelling the web. I knew that God loved me.

So this is how my story began, how I came to the conclusion that everything was my fault and it was because of the way I looked. This was to create a stronghold with multiple complex strands, which would not make sense for years yet; this was the beginnings of the anorexic season and the creation of a part called 'Nothing'. The development of Body Dysmorphic Disorder (BDD), which was the manifestation of feelings related to self-disgust and being unlovable, had however begun in much earlier childhood. BDD was another coping mechanism for turning bad feelings in on myself in order to keep my parents as the good people I needed them to be—it was safer to hate myself for causing all of this than to be afraid of them. My mind, in all its creativity, developed a mass of ingrained patterns of distorted thinking and destructive behaviour which served to distract away from why I was hurting so much.

Chapter 6

Though she may forget, I will not forget you

Journal Entry:

> *My mind is still running stretched on an elastic band—fluidity of distorted thinking that can stretch further out to increased distortions and feelings of nausea, or be indiscriminately reigned in to within normal parameters again. I can choose. I know that now. Her voice, and physical sensations associated with her, continue to be loosened this morning and dissociation feels like it's creeping in on me at every turn of thought. I feel like*

abandoning life and accepting instability, but know that God can and will use this. He can enable me to understand in such a way that through the management of these symptoms, I can become stronger...

But I'm walking a tightrope—maybe that's how it's got to feel, so as to thank God in all circumstances and in all emotional states, as this alone brings peace and healing. At the moment, the intensity of my feelings towards Richard, seem utterly unbearable, and whilst I recognise that these are also distortions of past relationships, it hurts because they can never be met...

If I could only learn to direct these feelings and thoughts towards God, where they would be met, I knew I would know fulfilment and every need within me would be satisfied. I knew that as truth, but the feelings were going to take longer to align with this. In the meantime, however, I held very strong needs to be loved by a mother, and a powerful transference dependence had developed. Evie was a child and there was no mother figure like she longed for, which in itself created its own destructiveness as these powerful feelings and needs that weren't being met completely got in the way of the work. The confusion came, in that I knew I was no longer a child and I felt unable to be the mother to myself that Evie needed and maybe couldn't ever be. Therefore, these strong feelings could never be met by me or by anybody else, and the risk was that, unless these emotions were worked through, they would continue to transfer into all relationships throughout life, where I would continue to seek out mother-daughter relationships that could never be fulfilled and I would continue to feel abandoned and rejected. This is the nature of repeating patterns of behaviour and, whilst I could see it and understand it on a cognitive level, I was nowhere near developing an internal compassion within myself that would help resolve these needs.

I knew that a complete God-dependence was the answer: that He could satisfy every unmet need within me; that He alone could reach into the past and bring whatever Evie and any of the others needed, but it required the arduous ongoing task of renewing my mind to bring these other parts alongside.

Gradually I became more able to control the symptoms enough to return to work in the NHS, whilst completing an NHS management qualification at university, and achieving several promotions. I had been seeing Richard for some time by then and was beginning to talk about whether it was right to start moving towards an ending. Claiming truth was as natural as breathing: I knew how to renew my mind, I was free of depression, and my weight was stable. Evie continued to cry out for mummy every day, and I wondered at times whether I would ever be free of this. Richard had helped me process a lot of what was accessible, but he had no experience with DID.

Whilst I continued to repress the details surrounding why my mind had fragmented, relapse continued to be a risk as long as there remained unresolved triggers within my unconscious mind. I still had regular nightmares where I would scream and lash out in my sleep. I had flashbacks and little snippets of information that I could not connect or make sense of, and this generated its own anxiety.

I found this passage in Isaiah 49:15 during another in-patient period when Evie was particularly disturbed and nobody seemed to understand what I was talking about when I tried to explain the children crying in my head and out loud through my own mouth:

> *'Can a mother forget the baby at her breast and have no compassion on the child she has borne? Though she may forget, I will not forget you! See I have engraved you on the palms of my hands.'*

Seeing God as a mother figure instead of as just a father figure was a turning point. I knew my identity in Christ, I knew that I was loved and significant, worthy, pure and blameless, but Evie still felt abandoned and no amount of renewing my mind had seemed to address that deep hole within me. Richard had told me that I needed to find it within myself to love myself, but as long as a part of me was desperately searching for a mother's love, this seemed impossible. Now I could find the mother in God and know a new perspective of God's compassion towards me and so, I reasoned, with Christ in me, I should also find it within me to treat Evie with the same compassion. I wrote the following prayer to claim over my life on a daily basis:

> 'Heavenly Father, thank You that as a mother comforts her child, You will comfort me and I will be comforted. I choose to believe that my yearning for a mother's love can

be wholly satisfied by Your love and I renounce the lie that it cannot. I will not be afraid because You will carry me as a mother carries a child on her hip all the way. I am Your daughter and valuable to You.

Be merciful to me, Lord, for I am faint. Heal me, Lord, for I am in agony. My soul is in anguish. Turn, O Lord, and deliver me; save me because of Your unfailing love.
You are a father to the fatherless and set the lonely in families. I trust in Your unfailing love; my heart rejoices in Your salvation. Thank You, that You have been good to me.

Please fill me afresh with Your Holy Spirit. Let Your light shine before me so that they may see Your good deeds and praise You. I will shine like a star in the universe and hold out Your Word of life.

Thank You that You are good and Your love endures forever. Praise Your holy name! Amen'

Therapy helped me to feel heard, but I had to make the choice as to whether I changed my behaviour patterns. It was hard to undo ingrained learnt patterns of behaviour that involved starving, but even harder to manage the thoughts, feelings, and behaviours of fragmented parts of my personality. They appeared to be triggered by stimuli that I didn't yet understand and wasn't prepared for, and they responded in childlike ways that were inappropriate to my adult way of relating. These parts were still part of me, that needed more than anything to feel safe, secure, and loved. My adult personality had learnt it, and I now had to teach it to the fragmented parts of myself as well. It meant learning how to be compassionate to myself in order to survive this: something that I had never known as a child. As I learnt it for myself, I taught it to the lost parts of myself as well. I would come to teach compassion to others as I began to understand the healing of compassion within every part of my being.

Chapter 7

Runaway 1981

MUM AND DAD GOT divorced the following year when I was fifteen years old. School GCEs came and went but I was too unwell by then, as remaining in control of my weight was a much bigger priority. Mum and I initially moved in with the man she left my dad for, but six months later he disappeared completely, leaving mum to sink into a deep depression herself. Meanwhile, dad married one of the secretaries who worked for him and started a new life without us in it. My sister and I rarely saw him, until all contact was lost altogether. I left school at sixteen years old to spend the first autumn months in bed, isolated from old school friends, and the rest of the world continued on without me.

Mum pushed me to get a job to get out of the house, which was extremely hard as I was suffering with extreme social anxiety, but I found a junior drawing office assistant role. The job was terribly monotonous, but I became friends with one of the draughtsmen and I started to talk about what life was like at home with a depressed mother and absent father. I told him how mum would come home from her secretarial job each evening to a drink and go to bed crying. She had locked the phone so I couldn't make any calls while she was either out or in bed, and there was no heating in the house because we couldn't afford it. Two weeks after I met Danny, he rang me late one night after getting back from playing a gig with his band. It was well past midnight and I had been sitting on the cold floor in the entrance hall in tears, waiting for him to call. That evening mum had been particularly depressed, and as Danny listened to me sobbing on the phone, he told me to pack a bag, as he was coming to get me. Two weeks past my seventeenth birthday, I finally got to run away from home—slightly later than planned as a child. I got in the taxi with Danny during the early hours, leaving no forwarding address, and disappeared.

I desperately needed space and time to recover, but I was desperately unwell. Danny rented a cottage in idyllic countryside, miles from anywhere, which should have felt like a safe place for me, but I withdrew further until I was not only unable to leave the cottage but became trapped within my own bedroom. I was unable to answer the door, or the phone, becoming paranoid that Danny was going to kill me while I was asleep. I hid all the kitchen knives from him and watched my back constantly, hiding under the bed during the day if anybody came near the cottage for any reason.

After six months of living like this, contact with mum was resumed and I allowed her to know where I was living. She bought me a cat to help keep me company, and I loved Clailea. I would watch her disappearing out of the top of a kitchen window to run freely through the long grass in the surrounding fields, and I longed to swap places with Clailea.

During the summer of 1984, at nineteen years old, Danny and I got married. It was a small, country wedding, attended only by our immediate family and a handful of friends. Despite my extremely low weight and emotional state of mind, Danny didn't seem to know what to do and it never occurred to him that I needed to see a doctor. Maybe I refused to see one, as my previous experiences of doctors had been so traumatic.

Mum had taken me to see the family GP when the school eventually rang her to tell her that I wasn't eating anything and had lost a lot of weight. I had lost two stone by then, but mum and dad had not noticed the weight loss, or the fact that I was skipping meals. She took me straight to see the GP from school on the day my teacher rang her, and I was confronted with an angry doctor who never enquired as to why I wasn't eating, but merely shouted at me for being selfish and not considering all the starving children in the world. He made a private referral to a female psychiatrist whom I visited at her beautiful beamed home surrounded by her horses. I was completely unable to communicate anything of the distress I felt and barely spoke to her during the time I saw her. My sessions with her ceased after the divorce and I was left struggling to survive within a shaky new membrane of my own making, after the family membrane was ripped away.

Danny was working inordinately long hours, travelling by train to London each day via a country service that was notoriously slow. My days were long and consisted entirely of battling with the obsessive-compulsive thoughts in my head. I stayed in bed for as long as I could, followed by spending the remaining hours curled up in a chair without moving from it because if I did, it would mean moving in the direction of the kitchen. There was only one small living area in the studio flat with a kitchen and bathroom leading off it. We didn't own a television and the obsessive thoughts prevented me from reading and, as I didn't possess any books anyway, there was no distraction. Getting up from the chair was to lose control because it would lead to eating; this would lead to feelings of guilt because I was so ravenously hungry that it led to eating everything we had, in an uncontrollable frenzy. I would eat until I was unable to stand any longer from the pain and weight in my stomach, before crawling to the bathroom to make myself sick.

When this happened, it felt like I was possessed by something beyond myself, a wild force that I was completely unable to control. It was as if I stepped outside of myself to look on in disgust and horror at the person who was stuffing herself with everything she could lay her hands on. This eating person wasn't me and I hated her for her lack of control and filthy habits—for needing food, and for putting it into a body that I wanted to deny and destroy. Another part of me was glad that the binge was so uncontrollable so that my encounter with food was not pleasant. This behaviour served a purpose in that it prevented me from getting anywhere near the reason behind what was driving it. My mind was focused on something other than what had happened in the past and whilst I still had to sleep with the light on, I wasn't in touch with the reason why anymore.

I hated the routine and futility of my life. The whole bingeing process could take well over an hour and resulted in feelings of total self-disgust and a sense of utter failure, as well as physical exhaustion. I would collapse onto my bed in floods of tears at the loss of control, desperate at that point for someone to help me. When I wasn't bingeing, on the other hand, I didn't want any help because the thoughts and fears associated with gaining weight outweighed any potential benefits as I could see.

It was the intensity of the bingeing that eventually took me to the doctors. I was terrified of asking for help and admitting to my behaviour, not least because of the sense of failure I felt at having not managed to starve to death after the length of time I'd been ill.

Asking for help marked the beginning of a new era and the commencement of what was to be a long drawn-out period of involvement with mental health services. I was referred to Dr Wood, a tall, slightly balding Consultant Psychiatrist from New Zealand, who lacked the bedside manner of my new GP, Dr Marks, but upon whom, nevertheless, I was to develop a strong dependency. Dr Wood began meeting with me on a weekly basis at the local general hospital where he would ask questions that never seemed to make any particular sense, whilst never proposing anything that might change my behaviour and feelings. Every week I returned and if he didn't ask me any questions I sat there in silence. This caused me enormous discomfort and confusion and I wondered why we 'wasted' an hour's appointment on a regular basis like this. I didn't know where my problems stemmed from anymore. If he was waiting for me to talk, where did I start? As far as I was aware, my predicament was caused by my eating disorder and I couldn't understand why he wasn't attempting to tackle that as I saw it.

I lived my life from one appointment to the next as if they were a goal to aim for, the only one I had. Maybe it was because nobody had ever listened to me before, or because I was so desperate for a father figure in my life, or for someone to take responsibility for me, but my whole life revolved around those appointments and kept me going, despite the fact that my anorectic behaviour was not changed in the slightest.

A report from him to Dr Marks at the time read as follows:

> 'Dear Dr Marks,
>
> Thank you for referring this young woman, whom I saw the same day at the out-patient clinic, 17 June 1985. I have seen her again on four further occasions, the last being with her husband. I should note at the outset of this summary that the conclusions in it do not at present add up to clear lines of progress forward.
>
> She is a daunting prospect in treatment for a number of reasons; in summary, these reasons are the rigid pattern of weight control she exhibits, the long-standing pattern of eating disturbance, the overlapping of eating disturbance with other behavioural disturbance and family conflict and, finally, the fact of her having carried her eating disturbance into engagement and marriage.
>
> As indicated, she has a very tight pattern of weight control. She exerts tight control over what she eats but eats so little that she is readily prone to fatigue, powerful hunger and a sense of being unable to maintain control. If she eats anything approaching a normal meal she feels gorged and fearful of weight gain, but still very hungry. On some occasions she vomits immediately, but on other occasions this feeling leads to her bingeing severely, followed by severe vomiting, which exhausts her and causes physical pain.
>
> At the present time it is difficult to see where this pattern of behaviour can be altered through any agreements or contracts with her. Further, it is linked into other aspects of eating. In a normal routine she never sits down with her husband to have a normal meal; on the special occasions when she does, this is followed by the sense of engorgement and vomiting. She takes time to cook for her husband. During this cooking she may begin nibbling, going on to

binge severely. She eats a portion of his meal but does not serve any meal for herself. The food that is hence acknowledged as 'hers' is a careful low-calorie snack diet.

As part of her contact with me in treatment she has agreed to keep a careful diary of her food intake, vomiting pattern and weight, which she has kept very carefully; as well she has agreed to note down her views and feelings during each day, a task she has again worked at carefully, clearly illustrating the inter-reaction between her weight and eating problems on the one hand, and her view of herself on the other.

Her eating disturbance began when she was 14 and she can date it precisely to a time when she was jealous of a group of girls who were sociable and successful and who were beginning to have boyfriends. At this time she felt overweight and wished to diet to become acceptable to them. After an initial attempt at dieting, she 'stopped eating,' losing weight steeply. In her efforts to maintain a low weight, her sense of engorgement and fear of gaining weight led to her vomiting, which she utilised as a form of weight control. Bingeing began gradually two years ago and part of her present acute stress is a feeling that this is now out of control.

The pattern of eating disturbance in the interests of weight control has hence been firmly tied to her own desires about acceptable weight from the outset, in spite of there being a number of other events occurring at the same time. At the same time, there was disruption in her parents' marriage (see below). As well, Beverley in the same year moved from the top of her class academically to the bottom. In discussion, however, none of these other events link to her disturbance of weight control, in the sense of providing any other way of looking at the issue of her views of herself.

As indicated, there are issues in the family that it is tempting to link to her disturbance. She is the eldest of two girls with a sister twenty months younger. Her parents' marriage broke up when she was 14, after a relationship her mother had maintained with another man for three years. Beverley says that she does not recall having known about this relationship until she became increasingly suspicious and confronted her mother when aged 14. She and her mother left to live with this man but the relationship broke up five months later when he returned to his own wife. She recalls her mother seeking to blame her father, so that she had little contact with him. He has subsequently remarried.

At the time of the break-up of the extra-marital relationship noted above, her mother was 'having a nervous breakdown' and she gives a convincing picture of drunkenness and hysterical behaviour, so that Beverley felt that she was 'leaning on me.' Subsequently, Beverley showed not only the anorexic pattern described above but also other behavioural disturbance, so that between 16 years and 19 years she started taking overdoses and cutting her wrists. She met her husband at this time and it was at his insistence, she says, that she precipitately left her mother's home when 17 to go and live with him.

Beverley understands this disturbance in herself as part of her uncertainty, shyness and being prone to easily losing control (in contrast to her sister). Obviously at the time she would necessarily have come across to the outside observer as being powerless and suppressed. As indicated, her behavioural disturbance outside the area of weight control has settled in the context of the relationship with her husband.

The couple have now been married a year, a step they took after 2½ years engagement because of their commitment to a house bought. He is a successful draughtsman, 7 years older than herself. As part of his success at work he is now working very long hours (getting up at 5 a.m. and getting home at 8 p.m.).

She regards the relationship with him as a close one and they were mutually supportive and warm to each other in interview. Overall, in talking about the personal areas of her life, she finds some difficulty in putting her feelings into words, or is easily overwhelmed by the task of trying to. Her strongest feelings emerge in her diary and relate to her distress about the particular situation of her eating and weight difficulties.

Her course in treatment to date is implied by the comments above. Hence, she has been able to give a detailed factual history, and there has been discussion about various aspects of the pattern of her weight control, although this has not led to clear conclusions about how she might feel more effectively in control of herself. In the other areas of her life it has not been possible to make clear connections between these areas and her weight difficulties, not surprisingly given the long-standing pattern of weight preoccupation. Beverley has shown a clear wish for support and guidance; as indicated, she has cooperated in the tasks I have asked her to carry out, in recording her observations about her behaviour and feelings. She describes herself as helped by the out-patient interviews, but only for a few days (in the sense of feeling more able to cope and less distressed about herself).

I will let you know of further progress.

Yours sincerely

Dr A J Wood
Consultant Psychiatrist'

Dr Wood enquired as to whether I'd taken laxatives at such frequent intervals to the point that I began to think there must be some benefit to be gained from taking them. Little was I to realise how hopelessly addicted I was going to become to those dreadful pills. Sometimes I dreamt of mountainous piles of shiny white tablets and even the mere thought of them became enough to make me sick. Eventually I was taking 135 laxatives a day and getting huge satisfaction in watching my body visibly dehydrate so rapidly that the weight loss was actually apparent within hours. As the weight loss was only fluid loss and regained once fluid was replaced, the only way to keep the weight down was to continue taking them.

Laxative addiction however is highly dangerous because it causes severe electrolyte imbalances, such as low potassium levels, that can cause a heart attack. Dr Wood didn't tell me this before I became addicted, and it was impossible to stop them once I'd started this course of behaviour; although as I was intent on causing as much damage to my body as possible, it probably wouldn't have made any difference knowing. With the size and quantity of binges ever increasing, as was my laxative addiction, it wasn't long before Dr Wood was carefully steering me towards accepting in-patient treatment.

I longed for freedom from the bingeing and laxatives, but freedom was not what I found inside the confines of the psychiatric hospital.

Annabel knew techniques that I didn't for losing weight and although I didn't understand what she was doing at first, it didn't take me long to work it out. I became aware of the fact that she was swallowing copious amounts of pills throughout the course of the day. When she realised that I had seen her, she threatened me if I reported it. She grew paler as each day wore on and one night I went to bed heavy-hearted, fearing for her life. When she surfaced the following morning it was a huge relief, which rapidly turned to alarm and disappointment however as I watched her consume more of the pills. As I watched her pitifully thin body twitching, I couldn't bear the burden of knowing any longer, in case she died, and so I had no alternative other than to tell and try to discharge myself in order to escape from her.

The other patients made life no less stressful than life at home, just a different type of stress. 'Animal,' as I named him, rampaged up and down the corridors hurling abuse in all directions. Several times he had come to my bed and tried to molest me, pinning me against the wall, asking for a kiss. I became terrified of bumping into him. Jim had the most horrendous scars on his forearm and was completely manic. Steve was a medical student whose wife had left him and he was perpetually morose and suicidal. Linda had a baby and was depressed. These were the ones you could talk to, others sat in chairs around the dayroom from one end of the day to the other with their tongues protruding from their mouths, their faces contorting in awkward, ugly spasms from the lifetime of anti-psychotic medication they had been given. Confused arguments and paranoia were commonplace.

Both my parents were interviewed the moment they arrived at the hospital to visit, and more than twenty years later when I obtained copies of my hospital notes, I was able to read for myself what was said during those interviews.

> 'Interview with Father at JRH, 14 October 1985
>
> *Mr Webber did not impress as unduly anxious about patient and was not happy with her admission, which he feels might have arisen because her husband finds her management difficult at home. He was critical of hospital arrangements concerning food and at the end of the interview I asked Sister to explain the treatment program fully. He sees himself as a religious man, concerned with spirituality rather than dogma and as practising his particular creed in his daily life. This does include being in touch with spirits, not necessarily ritualistically but more as an accepted and ongoing pattern. My impression was that he might be very firm about his views but his presentation was gentle and he expressed regrets about feeling he 'absented' Beverley after the divorce. He never felt she was alarmed in any way by the spiritual accentuation in the home when she was a child. Beverley goes to orthodox church. The family background is well documented in the medical record. There is one sister, Louisa, now 18, living with mother.*
>
> *Childhood: Schooling:*
>
> *He remembers her as a loved and favourite child. No worries about food. Mother had occasional bouts of dieting. No particular association with grandmothers, though he sees his own mother as dominant and the maternal grandmother lived with the family for some time. Sees no problems at school, had friends, worked hard. Parents did not know that she wasn't eating until alerted by a teacher that she was not eating at all at school. She left school without qualifications— 'lost interest.' He described Beverley, incredulously and unfairly, as 'not talented at anything.'*
>
> *Parents' Marriage:*

It was never what he'd really wanted physically but the couple got on well and he was surprised to learn of his wife's affair. He denied having affairs himself. He had known for some time before Beverley told him of her suspicions, and Beverley was extremely unhappy about the break-up, and father blames the development of her illness on the split up in the marriage. She 'went haywire,' went in for a good time, had affairs, etc.

Divorce:

He divorced wife when Beverley was 15, and is now married for 2+ years and very happy with Nanette, who is of Italian extraction, slim and warmly affectionate. At first Beverley stayed with her mother, and Louisa lived with Nanette and himself and Nanette's children for a short time, but there were difficulties, jealousies, etc., and she went back to her mother.

He feels she may well have envied Nanette her figure and indicated that she might have felt in need to be something like the woman her father wanted (my impression was that he had learned about this since that time rather than feeling it then). He settled into his new life without Beverley and since then has only second-hand knowledge of her illness. Indeed, he had thought she was improving over the last year—'it should have been upsetting, but somehow it wasn't.' He was 'disappointed for her.' He thought both girls should have elected to stay with their mother, who has not remarried and has been deeply unhappy 'like a zombie' for three years.

Drugs and Drinking:

Possibly one episode of drug taking. No problem with alcohol to his knowledge. Neither he nor his wife drink to excess.

Patient's Marriage to Danny:

They seemed very happy at first. He thought nobody had told Danny about the anorexia.

Father's Present Feelings:

'I handled it badly—she didn't contact me but I should have contacted her when we had split up.' In the last few months he has been in touch and been more demonstrative and open about his feelings. So far he has not had much response but feels it will come.

Summary:

Father's history of events reflected his early denial of guilt and ended with description of trying to re-contact and put things right—perhaps indicative of his newfound happiness and openly expressed feelings. Nevertheless, I am unsure how much he really forgives anyone, and certainly feels he has a right to what he has now found and in the difficult early period described telling Beverley to 'say it's alright with Nanette even if it isn't really' (because it should be—given his beliefs?). Hence, due to this attitude and her sexually promiscuous history, plus mother's affair, trust will be very difficult for her in either male or female figures.'

'Interview with Mother at DGH, 17 October 1985

Miss French is a plumpish lady who looked (and sounded when I telephoned her) very unhappy. In summary, she had an affair which eventually ended her second marriage and did not fulfil itself; her daughters cannot get on together, though Louisa still lives at home and she has had six years of intense worry about patient, with whom she has totally 'given up.' Her view is that everyone 'gives up' on patient.

Personality of Patient:

She described Beverley as always introverted, very possessive and jealous of Louisa, very popular at school, clever, 'having a rich imagination,' dominating, especially with Danny. Now like her father in that 'she never owns up to anything.' Basically shy, anxious, e.g., of telephones, hides under her make-up. Over protected by mother herself and her father.

Childhood:

Normal pregnancy and birth. A troublesome baby, crying a lot, bad sleeper until 11 months, a time when she also began to walk. Mother became upset through lack of sleep herself and needed medical help.

Ate well, never allowed to leave food and mother would induce her to eat a first course by sprinkling sugar on it. There were no scenes, she always then ate as directed. (Louisa made much more fuss.) Louisa also hospitalised early with skin troubles and tonsillectomy. Patient very attention-seeking, very, very jealous of new baby, who was born when she was 20 months and whose arrival mother had dreaded, fearing inability to cope with two children so young. Patient subsequently resented having to accompany mother to hospital to visit Louisa and got very bored there.

Mother's view is that she gave Beverley far more attention, because she demanded it, than Louisa. She also expected Louisa to be the jealous one and sees it as unnatural in Beverley. She then became very much attached to mother, screaming if she was left, e.g., at dancing class aged 3, at school later. Mother always met her and she screamed if this did not happen promptly. Improvement noticed when Louisa began school as Beverley took on role of protective elder sister. Louisa did not get on well at school, is described as unpopular and much less bright than Beverley, and often compared unfavourably with her by teachers. The sisters have never got on well at home. Louisa is 5 ft 2 ins weighs 8 ½ stone and is described as 'chunky.'

Events Leading up to Divorce:

Mother does not think there was any suspicion of her affair by Beverley. There were no rows, no arguments. She was surprised when alerted by her teacher that she was not eating at school. She realised that Beverley had lost interest in schoolwork but blamed 'music and boys.' 'She took money for school lunches, did not have them, then did not eat in the evening, saying she had had lunch.' Her husband knew of the affair from the start but did not want a divorce until he met Nanette. Mother cannot remember how the children were told of the impending divorce or by whom.

The Divorce and Subsequent Events:

Mother does think the actuality of the family break-up affected patient, and she 'went off' her father and did not really have contact until over the last two years. She had been having feelings against father's religion for some time prior to the split, was confirmed C of E at 14 and disagreed with father's very firm (and in mother's view, pushing and domineering) views on religion.

Pattern of Family Eating:

Mother: An unsuccessful dieter, weight watcher—gives up and decides she was meant to be plump.

Father: Believed meat to be bad for him. Consequently, often had something different from everyone else: he did eat chicken and fish. Mother therefore often cooked separate meals, first for her father only, then for them both. Father favoured health foods, Beverley had vegetarian.

Sexual Information:

Beverley had an early fear that she was not her father's child and mother has taken her to Somerset House to 'prove' that she is her father's child, explaining times and dates to her. We did not discuss patient's promiscuous period, the blame for which is put on the divorce. Mother believes Beverley now fears sterility and this newly expressed fear may lead to a change in her eating patterns. Couple have seriously expressed a wish to have a baby 'which would help.' Mother has discouraged this idea.

Early Family Pattern:

Like father, mother thought all was basically good. She was a strict mother and father's criticism of this was that sometimes she should say 'yes' rather than 'no.' Mother does not remember Father hitting the children, she herself sometimes did.

Mother remembers good family holidays, but Father and Beverley always together, swimming and running and getting on very well.

Beverley's Marriage:

Couple have been married 1¼ years. Mother feels they are in love. Danny is good and kind but not strong enough for Beverley who needs to be made to do things.

Overdoses:

Two at home: said to be 'because she is bored:' no hospital admissions.

Summary and Aim:

Individual psychotherapy long term to rebuild basic trust. She needs to know what is 'real'.'

No sooner had I returned home from the hospital than the bingeing started again. In fact, it started before I even got as far as home, as I stopped to buy food, ready for the next binge on the way. In relative privacy on the top level of a multi-storey car park, I started to eat with my fingers from an ice cream tub. With tears streaming down my face, I screamed, "Help me! Please God, help me!" Where was God? I questioned, because life just continued on as before.

I panicked over how I would cope until I couldn't bear the thought of it any longer and resorted to taking a large quantity of Aspirin.

"What have you done?" Danny demanded, as we stumbled out onto a street later that evening. With my head hung in shame, I confessed to taking the tablets. "This is just too much!" During the initial consultation and examination at casualty by a junior doctor, he enquired, "Why did you do it, Beverley?"

"Because I have bulimia," I responded nervously, thinking I was too fat to admit to actually being anorexic.

"That's no reason to die!" he retorted. "There are people in here who can't do anything to save themselves who are going to die, and bulimia is treatable!"

Looking at him with contempt, I thought to myself, "You have no idea, do you, of the hell I am going through?" He sent me to have a stomach wash-out.

Whilst the procedure was extremely unpleasant, something happened at that moment which I was unable to understand at the time, but which would make much more sense in years to come. The scene played on my mind as I relived the experience over and over. There was a perverse form of satisfaction gained that was to entice me again in the future. Maybe it was the fact that I usually retained such tight control over my body and during the procedure my body was under the control of others, an unknown experience in this form. Maybe it was because I hated myself so much that being abused by somebody else seemed to be what I deserved, or were they echoes from earlier repressed memories of being controlled that had been reactivated and were drawing me unconsciously closer towards them in an effort to understand and rework them? I'm not sure what it was, but something had been stirred within me.

Four weeks later, as a consequence of bingeing and too much self-induced vomiting, my throat was too swollen to be sick. No matter what I did, I could not get the food back up. In a state of hysterical fear and panic at the thought of food being digested and moving beyond my stomach, I swallowed another overdose of Aspirin. This time I knew how to get rid of it.

I went to a different casualty for fear of being recognised to get my stomach washed out. Lying, I told them that I'd never done it before. This time the nurses treated me with disrespect and scorn. They used a wider tube than at the other casualty department and forced it down with as much aggression as they could safely muster.

Whilst there was not the same satisfaction as before, it achieved what I'd wanted. I stuck to the same story that I was suicidal, because I couldn't possibly own up to using it as a desperate last measure for getting rid of food in my stomach. Besides which, it was far too shameful to own up to having eaten and not been successful at getting rid of it—although I had to bear the terrible shame of food coming back up the tube as they flushed my stomach contents out.

There was another precipitating factor not taken into account at the time. During the week leading up to this second overdose, Dr Wood had asked me to write a 'Fear Schedule.' He asked me to think about things from my childhood that had frightened me and to write them down. I had started to write down some of the occult experiences I had encountered but had found that I couldn't do it and never completed it. Dr Wood never took it any further, while I made a conscious decision never to mention it.

We were sitting close together in front of the fire with the ouija board balancing on the nest of tables. Me, Louisa, mum and dad. I was scared but knew just how important this was to them, so I buried that fear as far down as I could push it. We each had one finger resting on an upturned glass and we waited.

"Is there anybody with us tonight?" mum enquired.

We waited, the fear stabbing from within me. The anticipation of a response would surely make my heart stop, the pounding was so heavy within my chest. But another part of me wanted to see what enthralled them so much, that I wanted to share it with them. I wanted so much for them to love me that I had to be brave.

The glass jerked into life and slid abruptly to the word 'YES'.

"Tell us your name!" mum commanded the spirit, with neither hesitation nor fear in her voice.

Again, the glass came alive and with our arms and fingers stretching to maintain contact, it slid from one side of the board to the other, spelling out the name: 'A—N—D—R—E—W.'

I was merely an unwilling observer at this point. My finger remained connected to the glass but fear had severed my mind from my body. I was elsewhere, anywhere but there.

I was ten years old, where could I go from there except deeper within myself? Louisa, who was eight at the time, wore a similar expression upon her face to the one I imagine I was wearing. I could see the terror in her eyes, and blank resignation written all over her, even though she never spoke of it, ever.

"Are you *Saint* Andrew?" mum asked with marked excitement in the intonation of her voice.

The glass slid immediately to the word 'YES.'

I thought that mum and dad must be very special if St. Andrew visited them and talked to them like that. But we were not allowed to tell anyone because people would be jealous, they wouldn't understand, we were told. They wouldn't believe.

'Andrew' talked to us for a while, as mum wrote down the letters furiously while the glass swept across the board in rapid, almost aggressive strokes, spelling out whole sentences and conversations.

Later, as I lay in my bed, hugging my knees to my chest, I prayed the Lord's Prayer. Over and over.

Chapter 8

Car Crash

AN EVENT WAS to take place soon afterwards that had the potential of bringing me to my senses but all it succeeded in doing was proving just how desperate and determined I was to lose weight at all cost.

As was often the case, I drove Danny to the station for his early morning train, arriving before 6 a.m. in semi-darkness, the station still deserted. Danny, realising that the train wasn't going to stop at our station that morning, as was sometimes the case, decided we would need to race to the next station to intercept the train. We raced at high speed through the wet November roads, allowing him to catch the train before I turned the car around to head back to bed. Barely five minutes away from the station, as I swung the car around an awkward bend, I drifted across the centre line and into the oncoming headlamps of a lorry racing towards me.

I was going too fast and already struggling to negotiate the bend. In order to avoid the lorry, I turned the steering wheel as hard as I could, sending the car into a 90-degree skid off the side of the road and into a tree at breakneck speed.

Metal crumpled around me, wrapping itself around my leg; the driver's seat concertinaed into something unrecognisable, pushing me into the roof of the car whilst my leg remained trapped within the metal of what had once been the door. I tried to move myself, but it was hopeless. I had no feeling below the waist and nor was I aware of any pain either. Carefully I managed to put my hands under my bottom and lift myself up off the crushed seat to move myself a few inches across, but my leg remained trapped.

It was still dark and the road was deserted. The lorry failed to slow and had long since disappeared. In the silence I could hear hissing coming from the engine and steam was rising from where the bonnet had once been, now just mangled metal. I knew there were some houses a short distance away and so I screamed for help in the hope that somebody might hear, but nobody came.

Gradually daylight began to flood the scene and a young male driver was the first to pass and stopped, gingerly approaching the carnage. Realising that I was completely lodged within the metal, unable to be dragged free, he flagged down a motorcyclist a few minutes later and asked him to find a phone box and call for help. This was what we had to do in the days before mobile phones!

An ambulance arrived, followed by the fire service and the police. People were by now trying to get to work and the traffic began to mount up behind the ugly scene. Large cutters sliced their way through the metal, eventually releasing my body into the awaiting ambulance. I knew there was something wrong now as I couldn't move and still had no feeling below the waist.

After a very traumatic time upon arrival in A&E, it was eventually discovered that I had suffered a triple-fractured pelvis, and unfortunately, a spinal fracture at L4 was not picked up until several years later. There were no CT or MRI scanners back then, nor were there pelvic binders to help transport a patient with a suspected pelvic fracture from the scene of an accident.

The next fortnight was spent on my back in an orthopaedic ward as we waited for feeling to return to my legs. I barely ate during this period and being bed-bound gave me a break from bingeing as well as from laxatives, which was one relief. As soon as I regained some feeling in my legs I was determined to walk and go home. Only being able to stand for relatively short periods with the use of a stick could have been another opportunity to overcome my bingeing and laxative addiction but the compulsion was too strong. We hadn't got a car anymore and therefore the only way of getting into town for laxatives was going to be on foot. Despite the excruciating pain caused by vomiting, I rapidly returned to bingeing. The desire then for those laxatives was so intense that I frequently made the agonizingly painful and slow journey into town for them—completely unaware of the fact that I also had a fractured spine.

Dr Wood visited me at home every week after the accident. I was spending so much time in isolation and I longed for him to understand and take control for me because I could not bring myself to ask for help. So I planned to take an overdose before one of his visits in the hope that it would force him to take control.

Danny stayed home for the visit as he had become increasingly concerned. "You look horrific," he stated. "Your spine sticks out and is so red you look more like a dragon than a woman. Why can't you see it?" His face, unable to hide the revulsion written all it. Sadly, I couldn't though because I was never thin enough. Paranoia had crept back in, and once again, I couldn't physically turn my back away from Danny, even in sleep, for fear of him stabbing me. By the time Dr Wood arrived I was agitated, pale, and nauseous, having swallowed a pack of paracetamol. Dr Wood wanted to discuss alternative treatment plans and the way forward—Danny was insistent that something had to be done—whilst I sat, unable to communicate any of the pain I wanted to express.

"Where do you see your treatment going from here?" Dr Wood asked me.

"I don't know!" I yelled, taking them both by surprise. "Why can't you give me some antidepressants?" I whined.

"Well, antidepressants have undesirable side-effects and can be dangerous if you are not well enough, as clearly you aren't right now." He persisted in asking questions that I refused to answer, instead more preoccupied with the growing nausea and the fear of telling them what I'd done, and the frustration that I hadn't collapsed.

Dr Wood suddenly knelt down beside me to take my pulse. "What have you taken, Beverley?"

"Nothing! What do you want from me?" I eventually screamed, while inside my mind was crying out, "Please help me. Please realise what I've done. Please make this stop."

Dr Wood left and my heart sank because I had desperately wanted him to rescue me from the nightmare, but he needed me to ask for help and I could not. That night I was physically sick every ten minutes for several hours. The nausea lasted for three days before subsiding, preventing me from even thinking about bingeing. And there it was! The reason Annabel had been addicted.

It was obvious, I suppose, that, once it dawned on me, I would become hopelessly addicted to anything, no matter how dangerous, if it offered some relief from bingeing. Still, Dr Wood took no action, despite all the messages I was giving out of needing to be rescued. Inside I longed for freedom, for someone to take it all away from me. But ask for help, I could not. This would be an admission of complete and utter failure.

But despite what I presented to him, it wasn't the starving or the bingeing that I needed rescuing from. I longed for *freedom*. Although I didn't realise then, it was the past I needed freedom from, not anorexia—that was merely a coping mechanism, albeit a totally dysfunctional and dangerous one.

Car Crash

We were in the back room at Jan's (John the Baptist's) house. This is the room where I thought my legs were going to be severed by a guillotine. The curtains were drawn, and we sat huddled around a coffee table, each with a fingertip resting on a strange wooden contraption called a planchette. It looked a bit like an artist's paint palette, but instead of a hole for an artist's thumb there was a smaller hole through which a pen was inserted, the tip of which rested on a large sheet of paper beneath.

It seemed more sophisticated than the ouija board because the spirits could write whole sentences which we could read as they wrote, although it was hard to decipher. To me, it looked no more than scribble and I couldn't make any sense of it. Neither could I make sense of the fear lurking in the pit of my stomach. Stagnating, venomous fear.

"It's not mum's fault, it's the spirits, which are everywhere. I can't hang on forever, pretending to be brave and that I don't care. I need to escape. I need to run as far away as possible and never come back to this place."

I could focus on starving; on recording every mouthful I succumbed to. Proving to myself that I was failing with each and every bite:

> 5:30: cup of tea, one bite of Danny's toast.
> 7:00: cup of tea
> 8:30: 1 sweet
> 11:30: cup of coffee, ½ a biscuit, 135 laxatives
> 12:00: 2 cups of tea
> 20:00: very tiny bit of Danny's leftover dinner on his plate, cup of tea, small piece of red pepper, 20 paracetamol
> 22:00: cup of coffee

I recorded the binges because they demonstrated failure too. Vomiting was a futile attempt at ridding myself of what my mind was hiding behind the obsession with getting rid of the food. I had turned the food into what was bad and was driven to get it out of me, but of course it wasn't the food and no matter what I did, I couldn't get rid of it until I faced it. I ate so much it hurt and it had to come back up.

> *1 large bowl of cooked rice,*
> *half a cabbage, cooked with half an onion and mixed with*
> *1 pint of gravy,*
> *flour, butter, and sugar (quickly mixed together, pressed flat and grilled for speed), eaten smothered in jam and more sugar,*
> *1½ pints of custard,*
> *a packet of sweets,*
> *6 apples,*
> *7 Weetabix plus Shredded Wheat with 1 pint of milk,*
> *½ loaf of bread,*
> *several biscuits,*
> *2 litre carton of ice cream,*
> *1 ½ litres of coke,*
> *1 ½ litres of water.*

Sometimes I managed to avoid vomiting by merely chewing the food before spitting it out into a bowl, without swallowing any of the juices. Every waking moment was consumed with the misery of a mind obsessed with food and losing weight; a mind that was devoid of anything else. Anorexia was causing a significant distress that served to distract my mind from everything else, and to that end, it was a very successful coping mechanism. The reality, of course, was that I was exchanging one thing for another and still destroying my life.

Another short episode in hospital was to follow, with the sole purpose of giving my body a break from laxatives, bingeing, vomiting, and painkillers. As soon as another anorectic was admitted, I would discharge myself, as I was unable to cope with the competitiveness of anorexia. Every anorectic knows that they have to be thinner than everyone else so trying to get two or more anorectics to eat and risk gaining the most weight on a ward is a nightmare.

Dr Wood referred me to Professor Clarke in London at one of the leading units in the UK for eating disorders, where I was diagnosed with severe, chronic anorexia and would need to be admitted for several months. The in-patient programme required that I willingly handed over control for food to them and agree to eat a diet of 3000 calories a day until I reached target weight. I couldn't imagine ever relinquishing control to that extent.

Chapter 9

Punishment / Reward 1

DANNY AND I split up as the pressure became too much for him. He had started behaving erratically himself, threatening to drive us both into a tree to kill us, and getting increasingly frustrated with me. I moved back home to stay with mum, which was no less stressful, and there were endless fights over food. I was also travelling long distances by train to see Dr Wood and my CPN, whilst my physical health continued to deteriorate.

I stopped mid-sentence, trying so hard to hide how much pain I was actually in, but holding onto my stomach protectively. "Does your stomach hurt, Beverley?" asked Dr Wood, realising that I was struggling. I had stopped mid-sentence yet again trying not to wince. "Have you done anything on top of what you normally do that might be causing this pain?" he asked. I told him that I was still regularly abusing paracetamol along with the laxatives, but nothing in addition.

His tone changed. "Do you realise that paracetamol causes liver damage and you could die?"

"I know, but I just don't care anymore. I've failed at everything all my life. I've even failed at losing more weight. I've had enough. I *want* to die." I pleaded with him.

"It depends on how you look at it as to whether you've failed or not. Do you think you need rescuing from this current situation? Because the way you're going, you'll be dead before the bed comes up in London for you, and you may never get that chance. Do you think it might be sensible to be in hospital while we await this bed, in order to keep you alive? You know, it could be seen as entirely different and separate treatment from that in London, purely as a preventative measure. In fact, I could arrange for you to go to Oakbank Hospital immediately if you want. . ." His voice had an urgency about it.

"You're not putting me in that nuthouse!" I retorted, angrily. Oakbank was near to my old school and I had grown up listening to rumours of what went on in there. It was a huge sprawling Victorian asylum set in extensive grounds, endowed with its own church bigger than most town-centre churches, and a purpose-built secure unit, The Oak Unit.

"Well, you are probably nuttier than most of the people in there, so I don't know what you're worrying about. You can't choose where you want to go, or whether it's up to your standards or not. Oakbank happens to be in your current catchment area." He paused before adding, "When are you going to let go of the fact that you are no longer the little rich girl you once were?" His words smarted and were left hanging in the air, as if he had just stepped dangerously too close to crossing a line. I wouldn't accept his offer and returned home, hardly able to stand by then, let alone walk.

Punishment / Reward I

I could not pull myself together though and the following day I repeated the obligatory exercise of swallowing another huge dose of laxatives and paracetamol. By the time mum came in from work I couldn't even get up and was in bed. I felt very sick and everything was spinning. "Do you want to see anybody? Shall I call your dad, or Danny?" she asked. I think she thought I was dying at that moment, but I felt too ill to bother with seeing any of them. I had begun hallucinating, seeing crazy things like camels walking along the pavement outside the house. I was getting paranoid about being dragged off to Oakbank so I didn't want them to know how bad it was or how scared I actually felt.

As I lay in bed, nauseous and longing for oblivion to take me away from there, the tired drab furnishings began to fade, being replaced by the familiar and more elegant surroundings of Fernhill.

The group had gathered in the blue room and a young couple arrived with their baby. Daniel was wrapped in bandages, but his sad little eyes were peering out; a tiny lost person within the desperately frail body of a sick baby boy.

They came each week with Daniel to meet with mum and dad and the group, in the blue room, but then the visits stopped as suddenly as they had started. Dad said Daniel wasn't meant to live.

I felt such loss for them, and such guilt. Why had they come to our house? What were they doing with him? Who told them about my mum and dad? I wondered who had told them they would find healing in our house because there had been no miracle cures before then. I felt unsettled by Daniel's visits, but nobody spoke of Daniel ever again and the couple never returned.

So much fear, sadness, and emptiness that it's best to run away, to hide, and never come back here.

I became convinced that Dr Wood was going to send people to Section me and drag me off to Oakbank and so I refused to answer the telephone or the door. The slightest noise sent me into a panic, and I intercepted all the post before mum got home in case Dr Wood was trying to contact her and there was a conspiracy going on between them.

I listened in on the extension as I heard her phone Dr Wood, pleading with him to do something. "There must be something you can do!" she was almost hysterical herself as she begged.

"I know it's very distressing for you to see what she is doing to herself, and if it causes her harm, then there are measures that can be taken. In the meantime, I believe it is imperative that she accepts treatment herself for it to be of any value." This was supposed to reassure her, but instead it left her feeling as isolated as I did. How much more damage did he expect me to achieve before stepping in because I was in so much pain, physically and emotionally? Some days were so bad that I couldn't get out of bed for pain and nausea, but in many respects, those days were a blessed relief because I could neither eat or drink, and so the urge to binge or take laxatives diminished.

Since the night I had left Danny, I had slept with mum in her bed. Unbeknown to me, she often lay awake long into the night listening for my breathing to make sure I was still alive. On this particular night I couldn't settle because of the discomfort I was in, and Louisa and mum made up the spare bed for me, as mum needed to sleep. The following day I overdosed on twice the quantity of paracetamol that I normally took and went to bed praying for oblivion and death. But morning dawned and I was still alive.

"I'm so depressed—I'm still here—still lying in the spare room—being nothing. 'Nothing' cannot even die. Why am I still here? I even wrote a note saying sorry and goodbye but I am still here to see the fat—what do I have to do to die? I fail at *everything*. I took all the tablets I had, I didn't have any more, and I didn't even sleep. I want so desperately to

Punishment / Reward I 75

die. I'm never going back to see Dr Wood, Dr Marks, or Professor Clarke—I can't let them see all this fat.

Why don't I die? Is it a miracle that I survived? Does God hate me so much not to take me? I kept praying yesterday to let me sleep forever, but not to let me go to hell, because I am already there. But he's left me in hell—is this justice...?"

I didn't realise at the time that this state I was calling 'nothing' was in fact a dissociated state, a fragmented part of my personality, created to carry the suicidal anorexic feelings. 'Nothing' had been needed to take over for me at the age of 14, and she had a bad year ahead of her yet to manage for me. She was getting me further into trouble, whilst saving me from all that had happened up to the point where she had taken over.

Dr Wood had already made contact with a consultant at Oakbank Hospital, seeing it as only a matter of time before I ended up there, Sectioned, or otherwise. Eventually I did ask him for help, to his relief I'm sure. He confessed that he had felt like some kind of a king with an attractive young girl in front of him to cure, but as this had become less of a reality he had become despondent and disheartened. I was amazed by his candidness and felt a sense of achievement that I had not lost control to him. I did not anticipate that the next year was to be spent in hospital, or of the hell that lay ahead, or the fact that never again would I return home to Danny.

I was admitted to Forrest Ward, an acute ward at Oakbank Hospital, on Saturday 8 November 1986. I was the youngest on the ward and over that first weekend was greeted with plenty of comments like, "What a shame!", "Aah, isn't she lovely, so pretty!" and "Poor thing!" I managed to avoid eating all weekend despite a couple of patients pointing it out to staff. The Sister laughed it off, telling me they were merely giving me the weekend to settle in but come Monday, they would be coming down hard on me and the whips would be coming out. Frightened, but convinced I could outwit them, I waited for Monday.

Dr Lawton, my new consultant, arrived as predicted on Monday morning, his hair carefully coiffured, his hand never without a cigarette. In response to his questions, I tried to re-tell bits of my life and describe my current condition. Arrogantly, dismissing everything I had said to him, he announced that I would eat three meals a day the same as everybody else and tried to dismiss me!

"But I haven't come here to eat!" I argued with him. "I've come here to deal with my depression and to stop taking paracetamol and laxatives in preparation for going to London."

"I don't accept that you are depressed because you would have succeeded in killing yourself by now!" he announced, merely adding to my sense of failure. "Nobody can be depressed as a child for as long as you've reported and not manage to die!" he exclaimed haughtily.

Dr Lawton's own notes read:

> *'**10 November 1986**: Patient presents as a resentful, petulant, immature woman. Eye contact is minimal, replies to questions grudging and monosyllabic and she seems to have little idea why she came to hospital.*
>
> *Left after an unproductive interview, returned later to say she came to hospital to break the habit of taking laxatives and paracetamol, and for treatment of her 'depression.'*
>
> *Plan:*
>
> ➤ *Small meals, under supervision—continuing for 1 hour after each. Should not be allowed out of her room.*
>
> ➤ *Visitors to be advised against bringing her gifts of food.*
>
> ➤ *Avoid frequent weighing.*
>
> ➤ *Observe for 'smuggled' laxatives and painkillers.*
>
> ➤ *Dothiepin 75mg nocte*
>
> ➤ *Chlorpromazine 25mg bd / 50mg nocte'*

I took an instant dislike to him, but I had come prepared for all eventualities. From then on, I went into the dining room along with the other patients with a small sandwich bag hidden inside either a pocket or a handbag into which I discreetly placed the food from my mouth, managing successfully to starve for a further two weeks. The pressure of being caught greatly intensified and to compensate for this I gave up drinking any liquid too.

Charge-Nurse Henry returned following a short period of annual leave, clearly able to see the weight loss the others hadn't noticed. Whilst I denied it furiously, the matter was presented nevertheless to Dr Lawton at the next ward round.

"Well, what do you have to say—you've heard what Henry is saying? Are you losing weight?" Dr Lawton looked slightly nervous.

"Of course not with all this food you're giving me! I'm terrified about gaining weight because of what you're making me do. I can't cope with this regime at all." I chose my words carefully because I never wanted to lie.

"Did you deliberately try to kill yourself when you crashed your car last year?" he interrogated.

"No, I lost concentration and everything went blank."

"Humph!"

With a supercilious nod of his head, he motioned to his coterie with an air of superiority, inviting further questions. Whether I lied or told the truth, it would appear that Dr Lawton wouldn't believe me, but if he thought I might have deliberately caused the accident then at least he was beginning to believe that I was depressed. The interrogation continued, led by the power-driven consultant who managed to make me feel more worthless with every passing comment.

As I lay on my bed a few minutes later I was approached by a black-haired, long-bearded, and woolly-jumper-clad doctor who had been in the ward round earlier. Dr Rushworth strode confidently up to my bed with a big grin on his face said, "Beverley, we forgot to mention to you a few moments ago that we don't want you going into the dining room wearing anything with pockets, or carrying your handbag anymore." As my face fell, he about-turned and walked away. His face said, "Got you!" and thinking they had won, it was clear that he was delighted with himself.

I was trapped. For a moment or two I sat, trying to work out how I was going to get out of eating the three meals a day and quickly realised that it was going to be impossible. In a state of extreme anxiety, I searched for my key nurse to explain that it really was impossible for me to eat. "I'll go home. You can discharge me if you want because I really can't do it!"

Dr Rushworth was called back and together they tried to bring me to some alternative agreement. I was rigidly sticking to no solids whatsoever, offering to drink a cup of Oxo three times a day as an alternative to their suggestion of build-up drinks—which I wasn't having, under any circumstances. Eventually I managed to bring them down to offering three spoonfuls of anything at each meal, with a drink. It was to be eaten in a room on my own with a nurse and I was not allowed to go to the bathroom for an hour after each meal.

We were only a week or so into the new regime when Danny rang the ward to say he was being rushed into hospital for emergency surgery, which sent me into a complete panic. Danny had never been ill before and I wanted to go with him. We had a dog and a cat at home to feed and what would happen to them? Dr Rushworth agreed to emergency leave so that I could go home with Danny.

Whilst helping Danny and taking care of the cat and the dog were important, so was the need to get out to binge and take laxatives. In fact, it would be hard to say which was the greater need as the two were very closely interwoven.

I sat beside Danny on the surgical ward all day until the nurses suggested that I went home for a rest because his operation was unlikely to take place before midnight. On leaving the hospital I drove straight to a McDonalds where I bought two milkshakes, two portions of chips and a Big Mac, as well as stopping to buy chocolate. Upon my return to the cottage, I proceeded to eat everything Danny had in the house before vomiting and taking 100 laxatives. The hospital rang to say that the operation was finally underway during this frenzy. Whilst my head was spinning with thoughts about Danny and Oakbank, eventually physical exhaustion got the better of me and I drifted off into a fitful sleep around four in the morning.

The doorbell woke me the following morning. Mum had arrived to take me back to see Danny, before returning me to Oakbank, as arranged. I was shocked to see Danny lying pale in his bed, with a drip in his arm and a drain from the surgical wound. The operation, whilst successful, had been more complicated than anticipated. He tried to whisper to me about the details out of earshot of mum. I sat holding his hand for as long as mum would allow me, devastated by his appearance and the fact that I had to leave him.

Dr Rushworth was at the ward when we returned and as he rushed forwards to greet us, he enquired as to how things had gone. I cried inconsolably over how awful Danny had looked and that I had had to leave him there. Once mum had gone, his questions turned from asking how Danny was, to how had I coped?

"What do you mean?" I asked him tearfully, and naïvely.

"Well, I mean quite simply, did you binge, and have you taken any laxatives since you left here yesterday?"

He appeared to be sympathetic and caring and so, falling for this, I confessed. With the confession in the open and armed with what he was apparently waiting for, he insisted on weighing me. Since returning home and weighing myself, I knew that I had lost a further 10lbs since my admission weight and I was terrified of this being discovered, becoming completely hysterical in my refusal to be weighed. He was getting louder and more insistent, eventually calling Charge-Nurses Henry and Steve, and ordering them to keep me in a side-room until I agreed to get on the scales. Between them, they went through my bags and belongings, searching for laxatives, which they confiscated. As time drew on and I refused to back down, they eventually relented with the weighing but placed me under constant observation, which meant being followed everywhere I went. Unable to cope with this degree of monitoring, I ran straight out of the building and into the grounds, feeling agitated by the entire situation.

The following day I was simply unable to comply with even three teaspoons of food. I wanted to go out for a walk but they refused, saying that Dr Rushworth would be arriving soon to see me. On his arrival, he asked Charge-Nurse Steve to accompany us to an interview room for a chat. In a raised voice, Dr Rushworth threatened, "You have been constantly manipulative, taking the three spoonfuls to extreme. You are refusing to be weighed and unless you start co-operating with me, you are going to be Sectioned!" Not believing he had any grounds to Section me, I still refused to budge, insisting that they were being unreasonable and expecting too much from me. We continued to argue about the quantity of food I would accept and the fact that he still wanted me to be weighed until, out of sheer frustration, he announced, "That's it! I'm Sectioning you and that's the end of it! You're a risk to yourself as you overdosed when you were on leave."

"Laxatives aren't an overdose!" I argued, becoming frightened.

"100 laxatives *is* an overdose and could kill you! You have said that you have no will to live and so you are being Sectioned until you eat and gain weight and that's the end of it!"

"But I've been taking at least a hundred for ages and I haven't died yet," I pleaded. "I want to go home!"

"Tough!" and he turned abruptly to walk out of the room, slamming the door behind him.

Dr Rushworth's notes read:

> *'28 November 1986: Pt refusing to eat, refusing to cooperate with ward program*
>
> *took 100 laxatives while at home*
>
> *has very little insight as to dangers of not eating*
>
> *Plan:*
>
> ➢ *Section 5(2)*
>
> ➢ *side room*
>
> ➢ *restrict privileges*
>
> ➢ *to earn privileges, e.g. make-up, by cooperating with regime.*
>
> ➢ *She should also have to stay in side-room for toilet and use commode to avoid vomiting.*
>
> ➢ *not to come out under any circumstances till weight up and regular food intake*

> *to encourage to make decisions re which type of food*

> *To review Monday*

> *1:1 obs'*

He sent a female nurse to take me back to my bed, where I was told to change out of my clothes and into a nightie. She proceeded to pack all of my belongings into a binbag, including the earrings I was wearing and the rings on my fingers, my clothes, washing things, make-up, diary and books, before leading me down a corridor to a small side-room. It was then that I realised that I had been set up, probably from the moment they allowed me to go on leave to be with Danny, in the hope that I would do something like this. The room seemed to have already been prepared for this outcome: within it were only a bed, a chair and a commode. There was no carpet, only bare boards, the window was locked and covered with wooden shutters. My belongings were locked up elsewhere; there was nowhere to hide anything, and nothing to hide.

"Lie down on the bed and rest," the nurse suggested, as she sat herself down in the chair by the bed.

Rest! I had no idea that they could Section me once I was inside the hospital as an informal patient already, and I was terrified. As I lay there, I could hear a vague commotion in the corridor near to my room as an elderly man was trying to get into the male toilets. My nurse got up to investigate and the moment her back was turned, I seized upon the opportunity and ran for all I was worth in the direction of the day room. I had made a couple of friends—Rob, a ginger-haired, Scottish heroin addict and Marion, a middle-aged manic-depressive—and I was determined to get to them.

As Rob turned the corner towards me, I rushed up to him whispering, "Ring mum, *please!* They've Sectioned me! You've got to help me. Tell her to come quickly. *Please!*" With a tear-streaked face, I managed to scribble mum's telephone number down onto a scrap of paper Rob handed me before pressing it into his palm as the nurse tore around the corner in hot pursuit. Rob watched on in alarm as I was led back to the room, having promised to do what he could.

I refused to eat, drink, or take the medication once back in that room. I was told that I was on a punishment/reward programme whereby everything had been removed from me, even the privilege of using a toilet and having a normal wash. I would have no visitors, no clothes, no belongings whatsoever, and these would only be returned gradually as I began to eat. Meanwhile, the nurses would sit in the room 24 hours a day, taking it in turns in hourly shifts. I would have to use a commode and would be given a washing-up bowl of water to wash in their presence.

Angry and very afraid, I told them, "You can't force me to eat like this. You don't understand. My life was already hell and you are just making it worse. This isn't going to make me eat! I won't do it!"

"It will work, Beverley, just give it a go. Nothing else has worked," one of the Sisters pleaded with me. She put a screen across my door with an input/output chart on it that all the nurses were to fill in, recording everything I ate and drank. Feeling so humiliated by it, I cried with Sister Andrea as she sat with her arms round me, begging her to give me my make-up back because I couldn't cope without it.

"Is this the thing that means the most to you, Beverley?" she asked, calmly.

"Yes, yes. I will eat if you give it back please. I promise I will."

"Well, this will be the last thing you get back then. There aren't to be any compromises anymore, Beverley. If you want your make-up back, you will have to eat to get it!"

Andrea sounded so kind as she spoke those words, but I felt pure hatred in that moment towards her. Why couldn't she understand the emotional cruelty she was inflicting upon me, that they all were?

Nursing Record reads:

> '*29 November 1986*: *Beverley is adamant that she will not participate in any programme if she remains on Section. She has refused all diet, fluids and meds. Nursed on 1:1 as per programme and Duty Medical Officer informed of situation.*

> *Whilst Sister was sitting on the bed it was discovered that she had some make-up hidden in the bed clothes. She became abusive when staff took it away.'*

That evening when the night-staff came on duty the Night Sister came to see me in my room and explained a bit more about what was happening.

"You are on a 72-hour section while they assess you and come to a decision as to what to do next. Unless you cooperate now, you will not get out of here when the 72 hours have expired." As she spoke, she hugged me with genuine warmth, stroking my hair and allowing me to cry on her shoulder. She brought in a bowl of water for me to have a wash and even agreed to bring in my diary to write up, whisking it away again afterwards. One of her staff sat by the bed throughout the night with a blanket wrapped around her as I tried to sleep, although unable to shut out the terrible anxiety I was feeling.

During the course of the following morning, a commotion started up just beyond the screen outside my door again. As the nurse on duty in my room peered around the screen, I jumped off the bed, thumping her in the chest as I pushed her aside. As she made a lunge towards me, she slipped and fell to the floor. I didn't look back.

I fled the room, determined to get out of the hospital. Rob, one of the patients, was standing in front of the fire escape. "Open it! Open it! Quick! Let me out!" Rob fumbled with the bar, but all the doors had been locked since I had last run up the corridor. Hanging onto his jumper, I pleaded with him, crying, "Help me!"

Within moments, we were surrounded by male nurses, and as they tried to prise my fingers from Rob's jumper, I slid to the floor. Grabbing hold of his legs I kicked out, screaming at them, before trying to scrabble away, more as if I was about to become the victim of a violent crime. A scene in a film flashed through my mind afterwards as I thought about Rasputin being stabbed to death by three male nurses as he frantically and hopelessly crawled across the floor to escape. A sea of dazed faces watching on from a distance, fading into the background, each seemingly unaware of the horror I was enduring as our paths briefly touched at different moments in each of our troubled lives.

Ian, Steve and Tom fought to get hold of me and it was all over—I hadn't the strength against the three of them. Tom and Ian held my arms whilst

Steve picked me up by my legs and they started to carry me back to the side-room as I continued to lash out at them. It wouldn't have made any difference but was a demonstration of the little control I had left. I bit Tom's arm as he held onto me, screaming obscenities at them, to which Steve simply replied, "Go on! Scream louder if you want! In fact, you can have hysterics all day for all I care, but it won't do you any good because you're going back in that room whether you like it or not." They threw me down onto the bed as I screamed, sobbing, "I hate you, all of you!" They turned, and laughing, they walked away.

I wasn't aware of what had happened to the nurse I'd knocked over, as I was just intent on getting out of that room and escaping at all cost. I wasn't able to think beyond this, for instance, where would I go in November in just a nightie, assuming I managed to get past all the nurses anyway? I didn't manage it. I was later informed that the nurse that I had pushed had injured her ankle so severely that she had been taken to A&E and was subsequently off work for the next six weeks. Bizarrely, I couldn't even remember her or what had happened, only what they told me had happened afterwards. I was unaware of her departure from the ward, or of how long she was off work. Very little had changed by the time she returned.

Images of the hospital bed in that dismal, stark side-room, where I was imprisoned from life outside, began to fade and for a few moments I became aware of the office banter again, the telephones ringing and the printers churning out paper. I saw another email ping up on my screen. It was only another meeting invite and, before I could respond to it, I was drawn back to my incarceration at Oakbank once again. I was suffering with PTSD, related to the punishment/reward programme, and I would remain imprisoned in that room for many years post-discharge. I had been handed a life sentence with that Section.

I wouldn't look at any of them in the room, nor talk to them. I lay facing the wall with my face turned away from them because I had no make-up, tears continuously streaming down my face in silence. I had undiagnosed body dysmorphic disorder (BDD), and the removal of my make-up was a big mistake on their part, adding to the trauma they were inflicting. Most of them didn't seem to care anyway, turning up with a book or something to read, making no attempt to help me through the ordeal. Sister Andrea was different though—she talked. Throughout her hour shift with me, she pressurised me to the point of giving in to being weighed at last. Then to reward me, she offered a bath—a bittersweet 'reward.'

She led me to one of the huge hospital bathrooms where a bath awaited me, filled with about two inches of lukewarm water. She sat herself down halfway along the side of the bath, with her knees almost touching the rim, as she motioned for me to get in. Light streamed through the windows as I sat in the water, my hair hanging forwards over my unmade-up face. And I cried.

"You're having a reward! What are you crying for?" she exclaimed, as if saying what a silly girl I was. But nobody weighed me; nobody had known my weight since I was fourteen. Nobody saw me without my clothes on, not mum, not even Danny. Not a soul had seen me without make-up since I was fourteen. I even reapplied it before going to bed, creeping out of it early every morning to put it on again before Danny woke. This wasn't a reward—it was another punishment. I felt so humiliated and degraded. I felt like 'nothing.' Nothing could possibly be worse than this, I thought.

One of the nurses subsequently told me that Sister Andrea had told them that every bone in my body stuck out. There was an element of sick satisfaction in this, whilst also feeling enormous shame because someone else had seen me without my clothes on.

The Night Sister hugged me again that evening as I cried endlessly into her arms. "Beverley, it looks as if they are going to Section you again at the end of the 72 hours and it's likely that it is going to be for six months. You must start eating and co-operating with them because it will only get worse."

"How can it get worse than this? They are being horrible to me and I feel worse than I did before. I just want to die. There's no hope at all."

"You mustn't let them hear you talking like this," she pleaded, as she turned my face towards hers to get my attention. "Would you like to see Rob? He's been asking after you."

As I nodded, she got one of the other nurses to fetch Rob in quietly.

Looking rather awkward, Rob was ushered into the room and sat beside me on my bed.

"Rob, a minute, that's all, or we will all be shot!" the Sister remarked firmly, but with a smile and a twinkle in her eyes, as she disappeared around the other side of the screen.

"How are you?" Rob questioned in his heavy Scottish brogue, already knowing the answer. "I rang your mum, but they gave me such grief trying to find out what you had asked me to do. I wouldn't tell them though."

"What did mum say? Did you ask her to come and get me? I've got to get out of here, they're doing my head in and I can't stand much more of this!"

"No, no, she said she'd ring the ward and find out what's happening."

"Uhh!" I didn't want her to speak to *them* first. I just wanted her to come and get me.

Mum sat there by the side of the bed, crying. "I knew you weren't eating all they said you were. When they told me how well you were doing, I just laughed to myself because I thought they really don't know you very well. I knew you wouldn't give in that easily." I smiled a half-smile at her. "I just knew you were getting rid of it somehow…" Charge-Nurse Henry took her away to talk in the office about the Mental Health Act and tried to calm her down, which was a relief because listening to mum crying was stressful and it didn't make for a particularly pleasant visit in the circumstances.

When I woke up the next day, I changed my mind about not co-operating and decided that I had to get out and, if I were to stand any chance of getting off the Section then I would have to eat. I ate everything they brought into the room, trying hard to talk and be friendly with some of the nurses that came in, which delighted them. Whilst I wanted to get out more than anything, I decided that if they did re-Section me, I would not bother trying anymore. My reward for this: another bath!

At 10 o'clock the following morning, Dr Lawton, Sister Andrea, and Nurse Ian came to my room for the review. The 72 hours were up. I couldn't remember much of what was said during that meeting because I was so nervous, other than the fact that I told them that I would not cooperate if they kept me on the programme but would try to eat if they let me out and gave me my things back.

"Come on, Beverley, we've heard it all before. This programme will work and this is the way it is staying. If you won't agree to do it on an informal basis, then there is nothing else for me to do but to Section you again, I'm afraid," Dr Lawton insisted.

Suddenly Ian blurted out, "She told me she will leave if we don't give her her stuff back and let her out."

As I glared at him in disbelief, Dr Lawton sighed, "Beverley, that's it! I've made my decision and I'm placing you on a Section 2."

Once Dr Lawton had left with Andrea, leaving Ian and me alone in the room, I shouted at him: "What did you do that for?"

Shrugging his shoulders, he muttered, "I'm only trying to do my job."

Andrea came back to tell me that they were moving me to a different room. The new room was at the end of the corridor and half the size of the original one, with only enough space for the chair wedged down the side of the bed. Again, there was no carpet, only bare boards, and the windows had shutters across them preventing any light from getting in.

It was extremely drab and miserable-looking. The room was separated from the rest of the ward by enormous iron gates, which they shut and locked once they had moved me into the room. So I was now the only 'prisoner' on the ward and unable to run away again.

A local G.P. turned up to do an assessment at Dr Lawton's request, because Dr Marks was too far away to call in at short notice. He arrived, not looking too comfortable with the job in hand, complaining, "Can't we have some lights on in this place? I can't see a thing!"

"You'll have to ask Beverley because this is her room and she likes it dark," Andrea informed him.

He looked at me lying on the bed, totally unimpressed, and looking as if he wanted to say how absurd the situation was. He raised his eyebrows at me expectantly, to which I responded, "No! I want the light off." which didn't get us off to a very good start. I couldn't bear them to see me without any make-up, so I preferred to be in darkness. I had, by now, given up hope of getting out and so I lay on the bed, attempting to hide my unmade-up face, but answered his questions honestly.

"I'm afraid I agree with Dr Lawton, Beverley, and I'm going to be signing the papers too," he confessed before putting his notes back in his briefcase and dismissing himself.

Not long afterwards, two social workers turned up to carry out an assessment, another necessary part in the process. They posed all the same questions that everybody else had. "What will you do if you leave here?" Well, everybody knew the answer to this, and it would have been pointless trying to tell them that I was going to enrol at college, for instance, because they would have seen straight through it! I replied simply with the truth, "I'll go back into starvation," which was what I honestly wanted more than anything at that moment.

"What about the future, Beverley?"

"There is no future! All I want is to die."

"I think we'll just go and have a little chat with Sister Sam and we'll come back in a minute to see you again. Okay?"

Both of them got up to leave as I nodded, extremely frightened and feeling utterly without hope because I knew what was coming.

Punishment / Reward I

A little while later they returned. "Beverley, we think you are very ill and need control taken away from you for the moment. Left to your own devices we believe you will die and so we will be signing the necessary paperwork as well." They left. What was the point? I refused to eat, drink, or take the medication from then on.

"You've reduced me to nothing!" I cried. "This isn't going to work because you're only making it worse. You don't understand!"

Dr Lawton's notes read:

> *'**1 December 1986**: This morning she sits in a corner refusing to make any eye contact. Manner is sullen but she converses reluctantly. Still childishly defiant. Has co-operated with program and privileges are being rapidly restored. She admits, of course, that she is eating only to regain the status quo and announces her intention to resume her starving and bingeing as soon as she gets out of hospital. During the last few days she has binged, vomited and taken an overdose of 100 laxatives. Mother has been upset at the limits imposed on her visiting times. Patient has not asked to contact husband since his operation.*
>
> ➤ *Check with next of kin (husband) before deciding on Section 2...patient refuses to make a decision on whether to co-operate with program as an informal patient or force the issue.*
>
> ➤ *Check with AMH re pending admission.'*

The Section paper itself read:

> 'Joint Medical Recommendation for admission for assessment.
>
> We (full names and addresses of both medical practitioners)... registered medical practitioners, recommend that...(name and address of patient).... be admitted to a hospital for assessment in accordance with Part II of the Mental Health Act 1983.

I, ...N Lawton ... last examined this patient on: 1 December 1986...

I had previous acquaintance with the patient before I conducted the examination.

I have been approved by the Secretary of State under Section 12 of the Act as having special experience in the diagnosis or treatment of mental disorder.

I, (name of second practitioner) ... last examined this patient on: 1 December 1986.

We are of the opinion that this patient is suffering from mental disorder of a nature or degree which warrants the detention of the patient in a hospital for assessment.

AND

That this patient ought to be so detained in the interests of the patient's own health and safety.

AND

That informal admission is not appropriate in the circumstances of this case for the following reasons:

"The patient is suffering from anorexia-bulimia. She is uncooperative with treatment, repeatedly protests that she hates life and wishes to die, she has taken an overdose of 100 purgative tablets a few days ago and when she binges, the amount consumed is so great as to make rupture of the stomach a possibility."

Signed ...N Lawton.................... Date: 1/12/86

"She undoubtedly refuses to eat and will do so to her ultimate detriment—she doesn't care if she dies and says she has nothing to live for, and no long-term plans. She is mentally depressed. I feel she needs Section for her own survival."

Signed ...(GP)................. Date: 1/12/86'

Nursing Record reads:

> '*1 December 1986: Continuous 1:1 obs maintained. No diet taken—very unco-operative.*
>
> *Pt remains stubborn and protesting bitterly. Refused food and drink offered by nursing staff. Treatment programme discussed with Clinical Nurse Manager who advised nursing staff that pt must be reviewed by a doctor every day.*
>
> *2 December 1986: (am) To continue with present programme for time being. Continuous obs maintained on 1:1 basis. No diet taken, fluids taken. Ventilating her feelings towards the present regimes she is on. Still feels like absconding and not co-operating.*
>
> *(pm) Treatment regime of reward system discussed with pt. Beverley resents this and feels that we are asking too much. Taken small amount of salad and fluid then complained about feeling depressed and wanting to die. Ran out of the room and, hanging onto the gates, point-blank refused to return, screaming and extremely disturbed.*'

The Section was to last for twenty-eight days, five of which passed in that room and I no longer cared what happened or what they did to me anymore. The desire to die was a burning passion within me that never went away. I saw death as my only escape—from this, from anorexia, from life. I got so used to the routine and of having nothing, I no longer cared whether they gave me anything back because I knew I couldn't eat.

"If they hear you talking like this it will only get worse for you," Sister Sam insisted.

"How can it possibly get worse than this? I feel as if I am already dead and in hell!" I complained.

"Oh, it can get much worse, believe me. They'll transfer you to The Oak Unit if you don't change your way of thinking!" she informed me. "Dr Lawton is only giving you two more days at the end of which we're going to start tube-feeding. I think we need to knock the fight right out of you and lower your resistance by increasing your medication."

I looked at her horrified. I was trying so hard to maintain what little control I had left. What would happen if they sedated me to the point where I didn't care what I weighed? I'd get fat and one day I'd come off the drugs and then I would see what they'd done to me and it would start all over again because I'd want to die even more.

"Beverley, I promise to make this programme more rewarding for you, if you will only begin to make an effort to co-operate with me," begged Dr Lawton. "Professor Clarke says that he's very disappointed we've had to resort to such measures with you, but we didn't have a choice. He told me that the bed in London will be available soon. There has been a delay while they have been redecorating the ward, apparently, but it shouldn't be too long now; any day, in fact." He paused before going on, "Beverley, I agree with Sister and am going to double your medication and will begin tube-feeding tomorrow if you don't start eating today."

Dr Lawton's notes read:

> *'3 December 1986: Long interview—alone. Much more communicative. Accepts that she forced the decision on Sec 2 and seems untroubled by it. She does however feel humiliated by the programme of progressive rewards but accepts that her being treated as a child is the inevitable outcome of her childlike behaviour. Still feels her basic problems are 'depression,' feelings of inferiority, inability to communicate. Agrees to try again to co-operate*
>
> ➤ *Programme: bring forward use of bathroom.'*

Tube-feeding had always been my biggest fear as it meant total loss of control and there was no way I would allow that to happen. I gave in and picked at the food they brought in. I was so drugged up that I slept a large proportion of the time in the room, being woken up only for the food. My 22nd birthday was days away and I felt particularly depressed at the thought of spending it alone shut in that room.

"You're lucky to be alive for your 22nd birthday!" Sister Sam remarked.

"Don't be stupid! I argued, "I've been like this for years and nothing's changed!"

"No, I'm serious actually, Beverley. Dr Lawton said you could have died any day before we started this programme."

I just looked at her, speechless. Was I really as ill as she said? I didn't believe them because in my mind I was still too fat and wanted to lose more weight.

I began chatting more to the nurses as they sat with me, although some always came with a book and I knew not to talk to them because they were as uncomfortable with the babysitting arrangements. As I ate over the next few days more of my belongings were gradually returned, including my make-up. Once I got that back on my face, I allowed them to switch the light on again and open the shutters. It felt nice to be in the light again as it had been dark for so long. I learnt to keep my feelings to myself because inside I was screaming even louder, ever more despondent with each passing day, wanting to die was an inconsolable fervour. Anxiety was mounting as I faced the reality of weight gain being inevitable. My objectives were simple: stay in control as much as possible, prevent tube-feeding, get out of the room, return to starvation as soon as possible—die.

Dr Lawton's notes read:

> *'**8 December 1986**: Continues to improve—privileges being steadily increased and she is happy with this. Still maintains that she feels depressed most of the time and has no interest in continuing to live. Considerably reassured and encouraged by interviews but continues to maintain that she is depressed.*
>
> ➤ *Omit Dothiepin stat*
>
> ➤ *Start Nardil after 5 days.'*

Despite the regime I still managed to fool them with food. They really had no idea when it came to treating an anorectic. Every morning when my breakfast came, I asked to use the commode and the nurse would wait on the other side of the screen. With my shutters open and the window open an inch at the bottom, I would throw the toast out through the gap as quickly as I could. I always expected to get caught but it just didn't occur to them. As I sat on the bed one morning I noticed, with sheer horror, a squirrel running up the tree by my window with my piece of toast in its mouth! Looking away and trying to distract Ian with a conversation, he suddenly glanced up and noticed, "Hey! Just look at that!" he announced, with a hint of glee in his voice. My heart was thumping; he would suspect, he's bound to, it's obvious… He didn't.

As the weeks passed in that room, I told them, "Food is life and to eat therefore means I accept life. I don't accept it and as long as I want to die, I cannot eat." I was however determined to get out of the room, and so began to eat and privileges began to be restored. Soon I was having my meals back in the dining room with the other patients, allowed off the ward occasionally but still spending time in-between in my room with a nurse after meals.

Personal Diary Entry

> ***Monday 5 January 1987:*** *I feel very bad this morning. I have just an empty space inside—a big gap, meaning I am nothing again. It's such a horrible feeling —the only feeling I have, other than feeling very fat—which is even worse today after what I ate last night, so I went straight out after breakfast for 60 laxatives. I hate them but it is necessary when I am full of such self-hatred. Please take it away from me. Will these laxatives kill me? Why won't they? Why can't I die after all I do? By lunchtime I felt sick—so I ate a whole meal, (steak and kidney pie, two potatoes, carrots and three ice creams) then I was in so much pain. My stomach is so swollen and sore from the laxatives—I made myself sick. I felt like death and spent the whole afternoon on my bed feeling ill.*

By the time tea arrived in the dining room on 5 January—after I'd written the above diary entry—I was feeling very sick and didn't know how I was going to face the next meal, having taken the laxatives earlier and having already been sick. Reluctantly, I queued with the others, having to sit down in a chair because I had such severe stomach cramp. I was bent over double in pain and, as I held onto my stomach, my breathing sped up as I began to panic. I started to get frightened about what was wrong as pins and needles started to spread along my fingers and arms, then my legs and feet also. As I grew more and more frightened my hands turned into stiff, rigid claw-like shapes that I couldn't move. My face began to twitch and I couldn't call for help because I discovered that the muscles in my tongue and throat had also been affected and I couldn't talk. I was convinced I had caused a serious chemical imbalance as a consequence of the laxatives I'd taken earlier and was about to have a heart attack. I was terrified. Andrea walked in and swore.

"Somebody call the duty doctor *now!*" she yelled. "Steve, help me!" As the two of them picked me up and started to carry me out of the room, talking over me, rather than to me, I heard them saying: "She must be having some sort of reaction to her drugs, or something…"

Dr Webb ran around the corner towards us as Andrea and Steve were half carrying me, half dragging me along the floor. "In here, in here," one of them said as they kicked the door to a side room open. Dr Webb began to calm down almost immediately as he told me to sit in the chair opposite him. Andrea sat down as well as he started to talk, composed and smiling, at me. He was asking me questions but I couldn't move my tongue to answer him. Why wasn't he doing something to help me? How could he just sit there being a stupid psychiatrist, asking questions, when there was obviously an emergency to deal with? But ask questions and talk in the same gentle, peaceful manner he continued to do. Gradually the muscles in my hands began to relax, ever so slightly. After several minutes he paused and said,

"Beverley, I want you to walk back to your bed now and lie down and I'll come and see you in a minute. I just want to have a quick word with Andrea."

What was going on? As I started the journey back along the corridor I felt like I was in 'Alice in Wonderland.' I was clinging onto the walls in order to walk because the corridor seemed to stretch out before me like a long, distorted tunnel; sounds were echoey and seemed a million miles away. As I groped my way along the walls with tears streaming down my face and screaming, "*Help me!*" not believing he was making me do this in this state. *Help meee!*" The screams seemed to come from somebody else. Eventually I made it onto my bed just as Dr Webb walked in and put his hand on mine:

"You're going to be fine, it's okay." He was still smiling, which really irritated me by now because I didn't understand.

"I'm not fine at all!" I yelled at him.

"What you have just experienced is something called tetany. You *will* be fine!" he reassured me. I discovered later that low levels of potassium in the blood as a result of taking laxatives, and hyperventilating, causes tetany. I had been extremely anxious waiting in the queue for the next meal, on top of the laxatives I'd taken earlier.

Duty Doctor's notes read:

> **'5 January 1987:** *I was called to see patient because of disturbed behaviour. The patient presented crying, hyperventilating, and spasms with flexion of muscles of hands, adopting foetal position of body. Interviewed in office. She sees herself as fat, ugly. The patient hates herself. Suicidal ideation present.*
>
> *Management: Observation. Transfer to room where she can be observed.'*

The programme continued unchanged. Generally, I ate enough to be allowed time out of the room, but the sense of worthlessness and degradation I felt as a consequence of what I'd endured was enormous. I still abused laxatives when I got the opportunity to leave the ward and on one such trip, purchased razor blades as well. I hated myself with a vengeance and my thoughts were pushing me towards cutting myself because I felt so humiliated, ashamed, and worthless by what they were putting me through. I had not done this before, so this was a sad and new development caused by the degradation of the punishment/reward programme.

Dr King and one of the nurses held my arm up above my head in the treatment room to stop the blood flow. "You'll have to do better than this if you want to die!" Dr King snapped at me as she cleaned up the mess.

Duty Doctor's notes read:

> **'8 January 1987**: *1.30pm. Asked to see. Has slashed her L wrist using a razor blade. OE superficial wound 3 cm on L wrist. She said, 'I felt very bad because I ate too much this morning.' Felt guilty because she ate too much and didn't vomit.'*

> *'**12 January 1987**: 9.20 am. Slashed her wrist again, creating a superficial wound 3 cm on L wrist. Doesn't give any explanation as to why she did this.'*

Dr Lawton's notes read:

> *'**16 January 1987**: Little change; she feels that wanting to be normal is a sufficient contribution from her. Long discussion on her approach to life and her responsibility in her own recovery.'*

Chapter 10

The Goldfish Bowl

---

5 FEBRUARY 1987. I was finally transferred from Oakbank to the eating disorders unit in London. Oakbank had certainly kept me alive, but at what cost? I was not at all prepared for what I found in London and any glimmer of hope of finding help there rapidly evaporated into thin air.

I was confined again 24 hours a day within a small room: more pleasant than at Oakbank, with carpet, a chair, a table, and a wardrobe. However, the entire length of the internal wall of my room that ran alongside the inner ward corridor was an enormous expanse of glass. Other patients, staff, and visitors walked about the ward on the other side of the window wall whilst the anorectics remained in their own individual rooms. It was like living in a human goldfish bowl. I felt like an animal in a cage being fattened up—and for what? I had no life to return to.

I was told that I could decorate the walls with my own pictures if I wanted. I wasn't interested, as to me, I was confined again, back to washing from a bowl they brought in twice a day and having to use a commode behind drawn curtains. On top of which there was the food— a 3000-calorie-a-day diet! Throughout the day, trays of food were brought in and left. Every single item on the tray had been carefully measured out and was meant to be eaten, even down to entire pots of sugar and jugs of milk delivered with the cereal. Nothing could be left.

Twice a week I was weighed; being pushed down to the weighing room on my commode along with the other five anorectics on the same programme. We would be lined up along the wall on our commodes before being taken individually into the weighing room. I wasn't allowed to walk anywhere or use up any energy doing anything for myself, including not being allowed to pull my duvet back tidily in the morning. Hour upon hour went by in that room on my own. The same feelings of worthlessness and hopelessness overwhelmed me, along with suffering terribly with sleepless nights as they withdrew all the medication I'd been on at Oakbank.

I chucked as much of the food out of the window as I could, although with windows again that only opened an inch, it was near on impossible trying to chuck rhubarb crumble and custard out of it by the spoonful! Sometimes I just left the food on the tray, despite knowing this would generate a fuss.

Within a week, I knew that I wasn't going to be able to complete the programme. I was so traumatised by what had happened at Oakbank and all I wanted to do was go back into starvation. I had simply given up. Having brought a concealed supply of razor blades with me, that neither hospital had discovered, I lay on my bed cutting my wrist. The blood spread rapidly across my white nightie as I lay there with my arm across me, until it looked as if I had been stabbed in the stomach. And I just lay there... and lay there. The glass wall was about waist-to-ceiling height, with my bed positioned under the window so anybody walking along the corridor past my glass wall was unable to see me lying in blood. Nobody came and I wasn't allowed out of the room. It was some forty-five minutes later when somebody peered around the corner of my window and, instantly seeing the mess before her, flew into a surreal, silent panic. The nurse sat me on the commode, threw a blanket over me to cover up the blood-soaked nightie, and pushed me furiously down to the treatment room.

Dr Richards walked in. He was extremely curt and unpleasant and proceeded to stitch up my arm immediately without any local anaesthetic and without saying a word to me. I refused to give him the satisfaction of reacting to the pain, so I kept still, showing no emotion either, saying nothing and gritting my teeth. I was taken straight back to the room and told that nobody would talk to me in order to punish me for what I had done because I could not manipulate the situation to bring about more attention for myself by cutting! I would be spoken to as and when they dictated and not before. This seemed completely heartless and without any empathy whatsoever. I had no concept of the notion of trying to get their attention, as all I was trying to do was stop the turmoil going on in my head. It had nothing to do with them.

I cried alone in that room after they'd left me. It felt as if I wasn't being given anything to cling to for hope. I wanted them to help me with the thoughts, but repeatedly I was told that the treatment wouldn't start until I reached target weight. Surely something had to change first, because where was the motivation going to come from when I had none? How could I trust them that it was going to feel better after the treatment because until then, eating generated such extreme anxiety, with my mind telling me that everything was terribly out of control? At the time it seemed as if nobody understood and all they were ever interested in were target weights. My sense of worthlessness was being reinforced by their actions. I couldn't trust them, just as I couldn't trust anyone else. One meal I would try to eat but would then be thrown into such a terrible panic, so the next I left. My mind was in turmoil.

Where were they then? It was apparent that I was completely on my own, as had always been the case.

Dad came to visit one evening, threatening that if I refused to cooperate with the programme then he would have nothing more to do with me; he would disown me as his daughter! I wondered if that hadn't already happened several years earlier. I watched him in silence as he turned to leave and march back along the corridor to the exit. If there was anything to cling on to in order not to lose it, it would be worth fighting for but, as I watched him go, I knew there wasn't. Dad had already walked out of my life several years earlier so losing him again wasn't going to make any difference.

Danny's words were even more menacing than my father's. "If you come out of here the way you went in, I'm leaving you!" It seemed to be spelt out with such hatred in his eyes as well. I didn't care about Danny or our marriage any longer, and neither did he. What did it matter if he left—we had hardly been together for six months by then.

Professor Clarke was on holiday for the first two weeks of my time on the unit, and by the time he returned I had given up on it working. "You know how miserable living with anorexia is, and what returning to that life is going to be like. If you want help, then you have to agree to eat and reach target weight. How do you feel about this now?" he asked during ward round, surrounded by a number of people on his team.

"I don't want to return to the way I was living before, but I don't want to reach target weight either," I replied honestly.

"Does that mean you are not prepared to commit yourself to this programme?"

As I sat there with my head hung in shame, the whole room sitting on the edge of their seats in silence, waited for my response. Nervously, and eventually, I admitted, "No."

"I'm very sorry indeed to hear that, Beverley. I have no alternative but to discharge you now and make the necessary arrangements for your transfer back to your family and doctors at home."

Final Summary to GP reads as follows:

'Diagnosis:	Anorexia Nervosa. Bulimic variant
Contributory Factors:	Disturbed family background
Treatment:	Full anorectic regime
Progress:	Beverley initially refused to eat for the first ten days then made an attempt to start eating, but soon gave up and discharged herself.

Condition on discharge:	Profoundly anorectic
Disposal:	To GP and catchment area psychiatrist
Prognosis:	Poor'

There seemed nothing for it then. I returned home and Danny left me. Nobody in the world seemed to care or understand. Life was unbearable and everything was a waste of time, there was nothing to get better for, nothing worth fighting for. There really was only one alternative left. I had to succeed this time with an overdose. I went back to bed one morning after swallowing 70 Temazepam—stolen from Rob, the drug addict I'd met at Oakbank who'd turned up at my home after I was discharged. He'd injected me with speed and I stole a massive bag of the capsules off him while he was asleep. Having never overdosed on sleeping tablets before, I was sure that I had taken enough of something this time that would bring about an end.

Are they going to come and knock on my wall like they do for mum? Mum says that her dad knocks on the bedroom wall every night. Ken was killed in the war when she was a child and he was her reason for getting involved in the occult in the first place because she thought she could find him. I didn't want him knocking on my wall. I wanted them all to go away. It was all his fault that mum and dad had got divorced. She wasn't meant to be with the other man at all. He lied.

I want them to leave us alone. Leave *me* alone. I want to be like everyone else. I don't want to know anything about spirits and ghosts anymore. I just want it all to go away. I was suffering with flashbacks—flashbacks to my childhood and now flashbacks to Oakbank. I swallowed all of the Temazepam, put on my favourite dress to die in, and went to bed.

Through the fog of drugs I gradually became aware of Glenda, my community psychiatric nurse, sitting on my bed. I reached out for her hand and she squeezed it tightly. "Let me go, Glenda. Please just stay with me and hold my hand…"

"You know I can't do that," she whispered, tears flowing down her own cheeks.

A couple of days later I woke to find myself in bed in unfamiliar circumstances, with Clailea on the bed with me. I lay there nervously, wondering where I was, until Glenda came in to fill me in with the missing details. After I had been discharged from hospital she had taken me home to her own house. She had returned to the cottage to collect Clailea and now we waited for my GP, Dr Marks to call and for mum to arrive. Dr Marks got mum to bring me to the surgery where we would wait all day for Dr Wood and a social worker to come. I was sectioned again and the social worker accompanied me back to Oakbank, only this time I was delivered to The Oak Unit.

Nursing Records read:

> *20 May 1987: (pm) The Oak Unit. Admitted this evening under Sec 2 of Mental Health Act. Accompanied by Social Worker. Spoke in soft voice and said she could not remember what happened in RSCH. Discharged from RSCH 48 hrs ago prior to admission. Stayed at CPN's home last night.*

(Nocte) Observation maintained—very quiet. Temazepam 20 mg given with little effect. Keeps shouting and crying for her mother. Very little sleep.

21 May 1987: *(am) Waiting to transfer to Brook Ward—keen to transfer as she appears very nervous. Curled up in chair and rarely venturing out of it—withdrawn and isolated. To remain on OU for a couple of days until vacancy arises on BW.*

(pm) Mainly isolated herself—curled up in a chair. Refused to eat any solid food but will take tea (fluids). Very hysterical. Eventually led to a side room—Valium 10 mg intramuscular PRN given as instructed by Duty Medical Officer Dr King as Beverley screamed occasionally. She appeared tense and shaking.

(Nocte) Remains isolated. Had her night medication but with very little effect—awake most of the night, sometimes screaming and calling for her mother.

22 May 1987: *No outbursts of screaming—remains very quiet.*

(Nocte) Still isolates herself but a little more cooperative. Temazepam 20 mg given at 10 pm with very little effect. Very little sleep, walking around her room most of the night.

24 May 1987: *(am) Advised not to curl up in chair. Advised to eat breakfast which she refused—she is still negative about eating. Went out in grounds but did not stay long as she tried to climb over the fence twice. She was brought back in to ward. Not very communicative—she was asked if she would like to talk about problems and the way she feels but she said, "No. I want to shrink and die." Later she asked if she could talk to me, I said yes, but when she came into the office she said there is nothing to talk about. She sat for a while and then left.*

(pm) Pt still feels life is not worth living. Pt continues to refuse to eat.

26 May 1987: Seen by Duty Medical Officer—to move to Brook Ward.

Moved to BW—oriented to the ward.

Pt noticed to be missing at approx 6pm. Beverley had gone to the toilet at approx 5.45pm and no indication was given to her leaving the ward. Duty Medical Officer informed—missing person form completed—local area was searched and the area around the hospital. Police informed—NOK informed—Stand-in Nursing Officer informed.

(Nocte) Brought back to the ward by police at 10.06pm. Mood quiet and subdued. Duty Medical Officer informed, who said to keep Beverley under discreet observation.

27 May 1987: Observed discreetly. Remains sullen and aloof, curled up in a chair for most of the time. Poorly motivated and not initiating any conversation. Seen by Records and her Section rights explained to her. Minimal amounts of fluids taken today.

28 May 1987: (am) She sat sullenly all morning and was reluctant to enter into any conversation. She answered questions but her answers were barely audible.

(pm) Seen by Dr Lawton. Beverley appeared very meek, speaking in a low whisper that was almost inaudible. She was told very clearly and in no uncertain terms by Dr Lawton that she was behaving in a childish and extremely unsuitable manner and that it was up to her to make an effort to improve.'

Chapter 11

Punishment / Reward II

DESPITE EVERYTHING I said, they still persisted in punishing me in an attempt to force me to eat. But the more they humiliated me, the more they fed my sense of worthlessness and self-disgust, and the more suicidal I felt. I was unable to eat while I felt so low and there was only so much punishment they could hand out before it became meaningless.

Sometimes mum would get permission to take me out for an hour or two, but she would always take me somewhere to get something to eat! I would eat a huge amount and then excuse myself to be sick before leaving the restaurant. Somehow, I would manage to lose mum and buy a packet of laxatives and in my desperate desire to get rid of any trace of remaining food, I would dash into a public toilet and swallow the entire contents of the packet, washing the pills down with a can of diet coke.

One such day, following the meal and having been sick, I swallowed 60 laxatives before mum took me back to the ward again. I made the mistake of trusting one of the male nurses on Brook Ward. He had been making attempts to befriend me and I made the mistake in deciding to tell him how awful I felt at having lost control earlier in the day. To my dismay he responded, not compassionately as I had hoped, but saying, "I am really shocked and disappointed by this, Beverley, and you know full well that I will have to report this behaviour immediately." I lay down on my bed in the ward feeling bitterly let down, although I did not expect much to happen as a consequence of it, so I was rather surprised when I saw the Sister and Dr Rushworth marching towards my bed. It was hard to imagine Dr Rushworth was a real doctor. He was very scruffy in knitted jumpers, and his long black hair and bushy beard made him a very daunting figure. He seemed to revel in my misfortune and genuinely seemed to enjoy punishing me. My heart sank when I saw him approaching.

"Right then, Beverley," he said, "I am sending you back to The Oak Unit for two days to teach you a lesson. You will leave your clothes here on Brook, along with the rest of your belongings." He grinned at me as I looked at him in sheer disbelief and in silence, unable to hide the fear and disappointment in my eyes.

It was very late and pitch-black outside when two female nurses arrived from one of the other wards to act as escorts. A male nurse drove the four of us in the pouring rain to The Oak Unit. While we waited for the numerous doors to be unlocked, I got absolutely soaking wet standing there in just my nightie. As soon as I was handed over to the night staff I was led away and locked into a cell on my own. In a state of shock, I lay down on the familiar red plastic mattress, still soaking wet from the rain, and stared into the emptiness of the familiar whitewashed walls. Feelings of utter despair and hopelessness filled the room with the sense of betrayal I felt. I did not care what they did to me anymore, I told myself, because it surely could not get any worse than this. I was in hell itself, and nothing was going to motivate me to eat and get better, nothing. Nobody could be trusted.

Punishment / Reward II

Doctor Rushworth's notes read:

> *'**30 May 1987**: Beverley reported that she had taken 60 laxatives whilst out with mother today. Medical Registrar RSCH contacted by phone—advise no treatment except observe. However to transfer to OU. NOT to leave the unit even escorted til reviewed on Monday.*
>
> *Carry on with same treatment.'*

Nursing Record reads:

> *'**30 May 1987**: (am) Well behaved this am. Had a long chat with nursing staff. 1:1 obs maintained. No diet taken.*
>
> *(pm) Went out with mother. No diet taken—says she ate whilst out with mother.*
>
> *(Nocte) confessed to taking 60 laxatives while out with mother. Dr Rushworth contacted and saw Beverley. To be transferred to OU until further notice.'*

Doctor Rushworth's notes continued:

> *'**31 May 1987**: (am) Beverley's on hunger strike and refusing to eat. Therefore, only allow basic rights for living under Mental Health Act i.e. make-up is a luxury and must be earned by eating and not vomiting.*
>
> ➢ *1:1 nursing for 1 hour after meals even in the toilets – patient should be asked to empty bladder before eating.*
>
> ➢ *Patient is allowed to use toilet privately but meal eating privately is discounted.*
>
> *(pm) Patient says she has a right to her make-up but whilst she is on hunger strike it is imperative we have an accurate assessment of skin colour etc for her well being.*

31 May 1987: Interview with Beverley's mother.

Mother very upset. I explained the need for someone outside of Beverley to gain control over Beverley. Beverley's mother was also upset at the thought of no make-up for Beverley but it was eventually explained about her only gain being to be able to hide behind the make-up.

She (Beverley) was described by myself to the mother as using her body and starvation and overdoses to control everyone.

I also explained that once we had control we would also start teaching Beverley some social skills so she would have more appropriate ways of interacting with people.

Beverley's mother was crying when she left, but still agrees to support us in insisting on Beverley eating

Programme:

- *no make-up*
- *make-up returned after 2 meals*
- *Meals to be eaten under 1:1 supervision*
- *1:1 supervision totally for 1 hour after each meal.'*

Personal Diary Entry

Monday 1 June 1987: *Today was without make-up and was really awful. I curled up in my old chair and kept my head down. I neither ate nor drank anything. Dr King came to see me and told me that unless I start eating, I will be tube-fed. Charge-nurse Nigel asked me what the point was in being here if I was going to die anyway. I was so uptight that I just shouted at them whenever they approached me. I don't know what to do because I am desperate to lose more weight, but I don't want to return to bingeing and vomiting either if I am discharged...*

Dr King's notes read:

> *'1 June 1987: Seen. Has not eaten anything today, is very angry about taking her make-up away. Wants to remain in hospital but refusing to eat or cooperate with the treatment programme. To discuss with Dr Lawton.'*

Nursing Record reads:

> *'31 May 1987: Seen at length by Dr Rushworth and mother. In order to make some progress Beverley was told that her make-up will be withdrawn from her until she eats 2 full meals and has kept them down. Beverley appeared angry and swore at Dr Rushworth. Her sister, Louisa shouted at staff over the withdrawal of her make-up. Mother reluctant to agree but eventually did. Dr Lawton has been informed and agreed. Will see Beverley tomorrow.*
>
> *1 June 1987: (am) Has made no effort to eat despite removal of her make up. Sat in chair all morning quiet and withdrawn.*
>
> *(pm) Seen by Dr King re her persistent refusal to eat. She was completely unresponsive, only saying she would not eat until she got her make-up back. It was explained that she would only get it back if she ate. She reluctantly agreed to try to eat on the condition that she was treated for her 'inner feelings' afterwards. It was stressed that she could approach nursing staff for counselling at any time and that once she was eating we could better assess her physical and mental state. She agreed to this but when her meal arrived she wrapped it up and was found trying to throw it in the bin. She was then given a jam sandwich of which she ate very little and then also disposed of the rest of this in the bin.'*

Personal Diary Entry

> *I decided to try and eat to see if that would encourage them to help me, but when I did they were delighted, telling me that I would soon be well enough to go home! They have no idea. Nothing has changed. They still think the problem is the eating.*

Then:

> *I was trying to maintain control of my eating and my feelings, but I lost it and started to eat a piece of toast at breakfast. I felt so terrified that I just wanted to die. I cannot bear the sensation of losing control...*
>
> *What do they think they are doing to me? Why can't they understand? I am so desperately frightened and unhappy. I tried to cooperate and eat but when I couldn't cope with it, nobody tried to help me. I cannot bear being like this. I am not doing it on purpose to irritate them. I just want them to try and understand and help me. This is not helping at all—it makes me feel worse.*

After the punishment term was served, I was transferred back to Brook Ward again. It was at that point that I decided to start keeping back my medication under my tongue to save up enough to for an overdose.

Nursing Record (BW):

> '**7 June 1987**: *Says she feels she can't get better. Hasn't taken any visible diet today.*
>
> **8 June 1987**: *(am) No diet taken.*
>
> *(pm) It was explained that because she has taken no diet that her visits from relatives and friends are being restricted.*'

Personal Diary Entry

> **Tuesday 9 June 1987**: *I am sick of it, all of it. I hate them all, they are making my life hell and I have had enough. Now they have even taken away the little they let me have yesterday. I will not eat or drink again! They are reducing me to nothing and that's just how I feel; everyone can see just how worthless I am. I told them that this is not going to work; whatever they do to me, it won't work. My life was hell before I came in here and now they're making it worse. If any of them try to talk me round, I tell them that to eat means accepting life and I DO NOT. I reject life because I am not worthy of it. I told them that I have to destroy*

> *myself, although I don't know why. When I eat, I feel like I am losing control and the obsession and craving for food becomes totally unbearable. I have to binge and vomit to punish myself for it—punish myself for accepting life into my body, where there is none.*

Nursing Record (BW):

> '*9 June 1987*: *No diet taken. Says that she doesn't feel that the programme will help her. Her programme was discussed and the next step of privileges was explained. Beverley said that she doesn't feel ready to start eating because of the feelings of guilt she has. Said she's afraid of fellow patient.'*

I managed to keep some make-up hidden in a shoe under the bed just in case it was taken away again, and each day I put on the tiniest amount. One day it was spotted by the Charge Nurse, who demanded to know where I had got it from and told me to go and wash it off immediately. I was so cross that I fled out of the room grabbing some clothes off a chair and the tablets that I'd been saving, and took a flying jump straight out of an open ground floor window. I ran to some bushes, where I quickly pulled the clothes on over the top of the nightie I was wearing. A nurse started in hot pursuit after me, shouting at one of the gardeners to help her catch me. I had no time to do up the skirt and just held on to it as I ran, trying to keep it from tripping me up. As it became clear that I had managed to outrun them, the nurse shouted after me that she was going back to call the police.

Once I was alone, I didn't know what to do or where to go. I hadn't managed to save up many pills by then, but I took all the ones I had and the effect came very quickly. My legs felt like dead weights and I could barely keep my eyes open. I was found and collected and there were no kind words, they just went berserk. They threw all my belongings into bin bags, shoved me into a car and drove me straight back to The Oak Unit and dumped me there. I was taken away, locked up in a cell and left to recover from the effects of the drugs. I felt confused and lonely, crying for hours on end. With each passing moment I was falling apart a little bit further. I was dying slowly from the inside out. It felt as though there was nothing left of me but an empty shell.

Personal Diary Entry

> *They are all torturing me. They all hate me. As soon as I get out of here I will kill myself. I'm already dying inside. I'm forcing in food, forcing in life where there is no life, no room for life. I feel like I am not really here and do not even exist.*

Nursing Record reads:

> '***10 June 1987***: *(am) At 8.30am Beverley was asked to get dressed into her day clothes in preparation for attending Occupational Therapy. Nursing staff observing pt but got called away. Beverley decided to quickly grab some clothes from her locker and escaped out of the window and changed into her clothes in the fields and quickly disappeared. Missing person procedure carried out. Eventually returned to ward with nurse escort. Was asked to go back into night clothes.*
>
> *Dr King contacted for further management as pt had taken OD of meds. To be nursed in OU.*'

Back in The Oak Unit things were quiet, with few patients in, and the nurse to patient ratio greater at times. There were two staff teams each managed by two Charge Nurses at a time. One of those teams was managed by Nigel and Shane, a double act of unpredictable nature. Sometimes it seemed that they deliberately provoked in order to justify stepping in to restrain and sedate a patient who would be manhandled down onto the floor, with male nurses piling in on top *en masse*. They were condescending and sexual innuendo was a constant threat. I think they assumed that none of the patients on such a ward would see because we were either too disturbed or too heavily sedated, but I saw. I felt very vulnerable as the only female on the ward most of the time and they knew it. The pair of them continuously flirted, which added to the threat of being there as at times it was hard to know if they were joking or whether they meant it. There was no one to turn to for help, as nobody would believe a patient on The Oak Unit.

One month into my time at The Oak Unit, Dr Lawton, Dr King, and two of the charge-nurses interviewed me at great length, telling me that my Section would expire the following day. They wanted me to remain at

The Oak Unit as an informal patient. They said that I could have a certain amount of freedom restored, like going for a walk sometimes, but that the programme would remain unchanged. This bothered me and seemed unfair to be kept as an informal patient on a secure intensive care unit, and I left the meeting feeling frustrated and angry. They knew that they could keep me on The Oak Unit without a Section because I had nowhere to live if I left. I was still acutely depressed, and as I lay awake that night, feeling confused and desperate, I made my plans for the following day.

After breakfast, I asked to be allowed out for a walk, and they let me go, which was the first surprise even though they'd said it the day before. I walked straight to the chemist and bought two packets of paracetamol and a bottle of orange juice. Sitting on a damp wooden bench beside a deserted football pitch, I swallowed the pills in angry handfuls until there were none remaining of the forty-eight. The rest of the morning passed me by while I stayed where I was on that old grey bench. I grew restless, cold, and uncomfortable as the day wore on and the comfort of my old chair back on the ward lured me back. No questions were raised, and so I curled up and kept my head down, saying nothing to anyone.

Nigel glanced at me as he walked across the room before abruptly changing direction. Bending down to me, he asked, "Right, what have you taken and how many?" By this time, I was feeling so ill that it wouldn't matter anymore what they did—it would be too late. I smiled up at him as I told him the bare truth. His face fell and for a split second he did not believe me, before he realised that I was not joking, and a sense of urgency set in. As he rushed to the office to call for an ambulance, he shouted to the others, alerting them of the situation and calling for help. Everyone seemed to go into a panic, nurses were running, and it began to feel like a dream that I was merely watching from the side lines. I tried to protest about being put in the ambulance, but I was feeling so ill that I didn't care what they did to me. One of the male nurses was asked to escort me to the general hospital. Bob was an enormous heavyweight, whom I had never spoken to in a month of sharing the same living space, and now was not the time to get to know each other. He looked acutely embarrassed about being with me, so I eased the pressure for him by keeping my eyes shut.

The moment we arrived in A&E I was wheeled into a treatment room where they wasted no time performing a stomach wash-out. Bob remained by my side, not as a companion but as instructed, without a word of compassion ever crossing his lips. If they thought I still had it in me to run, they were very much mistaken. Bob waited until the blood test results were back to phone through to The Oak Unit.

The results were bad. A young doctor arrived at my side to warn me that it may be too late to save me and that I might die, despite the wash-out. His face remained neutral, maybe well-rehearsed as how easy could it be to deliver such news to a troubled 23-year-old girl. And, perhaps in response to the emotionally disconnected communications surrounding me, I remained silent, keeping my own face void of emotion. In reality I was very scared. A drip went up in a vain attempt to counteract the effects of the paracetamol.

Bob's expression never changed until the relief showed when they told him that I would be admitted and that he could return to The Oak Unit. The incident passed like a surreal nightmare. The truth was that I already felt dead. It seemed as if nobody in the world cared if I lived or died, and the thoughts that had plagued my mind before the suicide attempt remained as black and tormenting as ever. There was not a waking moment of peace within me, as there were no moments of peace within the walls of The Oak Unit. It felt as if the building itself screamed out with anguish and pain from the many tortured souls that had inhabited its rooms. I survived and was returned to the secure membrane.

Two days after my return to The Oak Unit, I could stand it no longer. I fled from the dayroom, escaping the eyes of the nurses in the glass office, slamming shut the cubicle door of the dingy toilet.

In a state of wild frenzy, I began to cut…

Chapter 12

New Beginnings

WHEN I EVENTUALLY CAME OUT of The Oak Unit, I initially moved back in with mum. Danny and I had got divorced during the time I was inside, and I discovered that he had been seeing somebody for some time before I had even gone to the London eating disorders unit. He had continued to visit during my hospital admission, causing continuous confusion over the divorce proceedings whilst I remained ignorant about the other person. He would take me home, help me run away several times, beg me to rethink the divorce, but in my mind, he'd already chosen to leave, as had dad, and it was over.

Once home, I returned to starvation and any weight gained was quickly lost again. Out of the blue, I received a phone call from an old school friend, whom I hadn't seen or heard from for years, and we met up. She invited me to go with her to her church to ask for help and, despite believing I was totally beyond help, I agreed to go with her. I was enjoying having her friendship back in my life, and so went to church—for her sake, not for mine.

At the end of the service she left me in my seat while she went to ask her church leader for help. I didn't take much notice of it because I thought it a waste of time, but her minister arranged for us both to see an elder's wife the following day. In the morning I willingly accompanied her but with no expectation of there being any help to be found. I was asked to sit in a chair in the middle of the lounge while two women, and my friend, stood around me praying for me. After 45 mins or so, they paused and asked me if I wanted to ask Jesus into my life. I felt a bit confused by this at the time because I thought I'd already done that when I was a child, but I didn't argue with them and followed them in a simple prayer, renewing the commitment I'd made ten years earlier. They then asked me if I would say sorry to God for all the sin in my life. Anger rose in me as I thought instead about all the sin inflicted upon me, but I found myself instead, following their very simple repentance prayer.

In an instant, I felt oppression and despair lifted off me like a heavy black blanket. This was something that I had not anticipated when I had gone that afternoon, and would not have dared risking having any expectation of, but I nevertheless received a miracle. Although I had a long fight ahead of me to get well, I now wanted to get better and knew that I had been healed to live and that I could walk free. The church provided intensive support during the first few months of my recovery, moving me into live with a young family within the church. I had very strict boundaries put in place for my protection but these were not the harsh boundaries of the punishment/reward programme, but ones within which I felt loved and safe for the first time in my life. Life was an adventure as I started out towards recovery, knowing finally that God had a future and a hope for me.

A consultant surgeon at the church provided me with work experience as a medical secretary working alongside his own secretary, which eventually led to a permanent role some months later at the local general hospital. I was, however, deeply traumatised by my in-patient experiences the year before, and so it is quite incredible now to reflect back on this move to working within the NHS in a role where I was surrounded by doctors.

My experience of doctors were that they took control and implemented punishment in order to then reward with something taken for granted by everybody else as a basic human right. The whole concept of the term *'punishment/reward,'* the name given to the treatment for anorexia that I received back then, was another one of those opposing conflicting experiences of good and evil that I had grown up experiencing. I was about to step into another one of these double-bind experiences when a junior doctor within the anaesthetics department I was working for, began sexually abusing me. I was so conditioned to do what I was told and not to tell anybody, and used to doctors controlling my life so they could do whatever they wanted to me, that I felt completely powerless to stop it. Once again, I was unable to find a voice to summon help, whilst spending my days surrounded by people who were caring for others.

I tried really hard to get my life back on track with the support of the church. Slowly over time I began eating more regularly and stopped abusing laxatives. Whilst progress was clearly being made, I became extremely depressed as my emotions began to return to a more conscious level as weight went back on. I felt ugly and disgusting, which had such a powerful hold over me that it was simply hard to face being me, a person who wasn't anorectic. I had lost my identity. Who was I anyway without anorexia? I was still somebody that others controlled and had no identity of my own. How would I ever see my body as God-given, wonderfully and fearfully made, when it took so much punishment from the hands of those driven by their own distorted minds to hurt and control me, including my own?

Finally, having given up on trying to deal with it spiritually, I registered with a new doctor and told him that I was hearing voices and was obsessed with death. I did not tell him that I was being abused at the hospital by one of the doctors I worked with, or of the confusion, the fear, and the isolation this was causing; I didn't tell anybody about the enormous conflict I was fighting between trying to recover whilst I continued being controlled and humiliated. I did not tell him about the punishment/reward programme—I had no idea that I was in fact suffering from post-traumatic stress disorder after what had happened at Oakbank the previous year, compounded and reinforced now by what was going on in my work-place. I had no concept of the fact that none of this was my fault, because I had simply been brainwashed into being, and behaving as, a victim.

Not surprisingly however, I was admitted that evening to a new psychiatric hospital where they had never heard of me, so neither did they know where I'd been or what I'd been through. Repeating the pattern at Oakbank, I told them nothing of my childhood or the current experiences, because I had no idea how to communicate the confusion and distress I was feeling. I had never had a voice, and it would be years before I found it.

The question as to how I should behave as a patient now that I wasn't anorectic tormented me because I had no other way of expressing the pain I was in. How could I convince them of the desperate need to rid myself of all that was within me; the thoughts driving me to hopelessness and the constant urge to escape that I'd been battling without comprehension since childhood, if there were no outward symptoms of illness—at least as I perceived it? What was wrong with me? They clearly didn't see me as psychotic, but the church hadn't been able to stop the thoughts either. Hospitals were a place where you got hurt, not cared for anyway, where you were punished before they could reward you with a cure that was *inflicted* upon you; and I was going to make it as difficult for them as it was for me. It wasn't long before I found myself Sectioned again, and control was yet again taken away from me.

Days were long and boring with strange conversations between some of the other more rational patients I tried to strike up some sort of a relationship with in order to survive, but it was unpleasant and tough. One man my age used to spend his days sitting on the floor of a seldom-used room on his own and every time I walked through he would begin masturbating. Another man I had initially assumed was a safe bet, had in fact attempted to strangle his mother. Another, an architect, with such a handsome face, had thrown himself onto some sort of machete that he'd managed to stand upright into the ground. He appeared for breakfast one day with a shirt tied around his head after shaving off all his hair during the night and started telling everybody I was having his child! I continued to fight the desire to kill myself, without any knowledge or understanding of what it was that was driving me to feel like this, as I remained disconnected from other aspects of my life, past and present.

New Beginnings

Feeling torn between the 'security' the Section offered, and the terrible fear of losing control again to another doctor, I rang my mum and insisted that she had the Section annulled and demanded my discharge. This she did, and I returned once again to what had become a very lonely and isolated existence, typing Pain Clinic letters during the day for a different set of doctors, and being abused by another one of them. I felt like I was going mad, madder in fact than I'd ever felt before as an anorectic. And was it any surprise? When I was anorectic, doctors were associated with giving care, even if that was unpleasant; now however they were also my colleagues, my friends at church, and now one, a sexual predator. Life seemed to have a habit of repeating itself.

I would turn up at a mid-week church housegroup but I couldn't concentrate and felt a million miles away from everyone and normal life. My life felt so bizarre compared to everybody else's and my intense thoughts and feelings isolated me and prevented me from making normal friendships with people of my own age. I wasn't really aware of anybody else in the housegroup, so when Paul asked me if I would accompany him to his company dinner, I saw him for the first time, even though I'd been sitting on a settee with him in somebody's lounge for some time by then. I would not have been able to identify anyone in that group if I met them outside of it. I was missing so much of life due to the stress of what I was going through, and from my own disordered thinking and horrendous depression.

Paul had become a Christian at about the same time as me and had been present when I'd given my testimony and been baptised after the initial healing, so there was nothing to hide from him. He arrived to take me out, and as he opened the car door for me I saw a small gift-wrapped present on the passenger seat. I wasn't used to being treated like this and several more dates were to follow. He didn't discuss my past, nor did he comment on my weight, my make-up or my clothes; he didn't try to take advantage of me, treating me with respect and as a companion. In Paul, I was to find a partner for life who could be totally and completely trusted, no matter what I threw at him.

Despite this new friendship, I remained severely depressed and was admitted back to the hospital yet again for further treatment. I had gained three and a half stone since my last admission and a rather self-assured junior psychiatrist, who recognised me from my last admission, arrived to go through the usual admission procedure, and said "What on earth have you done to yourself?" as he looked at me—with the same disgust I felt about myself, it seemed. I felt the colour flood to my cheeks. So, I must be fat! The thought hit me like a brick out of nowhere because I had tried so hard to ignore it and I really had no idea what I looked like. The thought that I was disgusting overwhelmed me, and self-loathing and shame hit really hard.

This time they performed electro-convulsive therapy, ECT. Treatment occurred twice weekly when an anaesthetist from the department that I worked in at the general hospital would arrive to assist, much to my enormous embarrassment and more confusion surrounding doctors. Yet again the familiar theme of punishment/reward was imprinted into my mind as a reinforcement. On the morning of the treatment, patients from various wards around the hospital would be rounded up in a minibus and driven to a newer building where the ECT machine was kept. This was a new dimension of degradation and humiliation. Half a dozen or so patients would be taken to a room and left to wait their turn. I was the only young person being given this treatment at the time and I would sit there looking around at elderly disturbed patients, who didn't seem to have a clue what was happening to them, and thinking how I longed to be even less aware of what was happening to me as well, unaware of the fact that I was in fact so completely disconnected from what had brought me to this point in my life that I was no different to them in many respects. It would take me years to allow it into consciousness but for the moment, this period of my life was about to be wiped out forever.

"Beverley, can you come through now, please?" a nurse called from around the doorway. I followed her out into the corridor and into an area where there were several dishevelled beds with rather unclean looking sheets strewn across them. "Lie down on the bed here and I'll be back in a minute for you when they're ready." As she disappeared through another door, I tried not to think about who might have been in the bed before me as I lay down on it. A few minutes later I was pushed on the bed into another room where one of my colleagues waited, along with the junior psychiatrist who had admitted me.

"Hi Beverley, how are you?" smiled the doctor I recognised from work.

"Oh, I'm fine, thank you, how are you?" I answered automatically, feeling acutely embarrassed because I clearly wasn't fine at all. The psychiatrist was standing behind my head at the end of the bed with an electric cable in each hand as I tried desperately hard to blot him, and what he was going to do to me, out of my thoughts.

"I'm going to be sick," I thought from absolute terror, but as the anaesthetic raced up my arm, I drifted away and was otherwise unaware of anything else that happened to me afterwards in that room. *Punishment reward. Punishment reward.*

When I woke up my head was hurting like hell. I don't remember being taken back in the minibus each time after that but I went twice a week for several weeks. After every treatment I was put to bed in a side room back on my own ward to sleep off the effects of the anaesthetic and the headache. Paul would arrive each day after work but I have no memory whatsoever of anything during this period. The ECT caused permanent short-term memory loss. Friends from church visited me but I have no recollection of them. Paul would be allowed to take me out sometimes and he took me out to visit various friends of his that I was sometimes being introduced to for the first time, but then I couldn't remember ever having met them before. He recalls turning up to find me with dull red circles imprinted on my temples, which he found unsettling.

What it didn't do was wipe out traumatic memories, which might have proved more useful, or cure me of my depression, which remained steadfast. Apart from discovering that I couldn't remember anything from that period in my life after the first dose of ECT, it achieved nothing. Once again, I was released back into society to contemplate where I went next. How was I going to survive like this? How much more could I take? I knew that God wouldn't leave me like this—that he would complete the good work he had begun in me. I had to believe it for all I was worth. There had to be a reason for this, there just had to be. There had to be some reward for all the punishment so far but I was struggling to find it—and looking in all the wrong places.

Chapter 13

Blessings

I didn't know if I would ever be capable of love, but I didn't want Paul to leave me either. There was something about him that made me feel safe; I had never felt safe or been able to trust anybody before, so I had to make sure he was going to be there for me when I came home after being admitted back to the eating disorders unit in London to see if they could make sense of what was happening to me (they couldn't help).

"Paul, are you going to stay with me forever?" I blurted out during one particular trek up to London to see me. I don't think he knew how to reply, other than to ask me why I wanted to know all of a sudden. After he left, I really had no idea as to whether or not he would come back after that, but later that evening he returned again, bringing with him an engagement ring. Before the year was out, we were married and expecting a baby. There was suddenly so much to fight for, so much worth getting better for. Paul arranged for private psychiatric treatment for me throughout the pregnancy, some of which was spent back in hospital under the new psychiatrist's care. I was listened to and treated well at the small private clinic at 11 Glebe Road, Reading. But people were scared—could I look after a baby? And, what about love? I wanted this baby and I wanted so much to be able to love but I didn't know the first thing about love.

Nicholas was born on 7 May 1991. As I held him in my arms for the first time I felt my heart would burst with love for him. I was so amazed to find that my heart was even capable of experiencing anything other than despair and pain. "Thank you, Jesus," I cried. "Thank you for saving me, thank you for giving me Paul and thank you for this miracle as well, for giving me a son." At last stability seemed to be within reach.

Sixteen months later, God brought along another miracle for us and we called him Jonathon James. Here, at last, were two very real positive 'rewards.'

I knew from the moment that I had experienced the first stage in my healing that there was a purpose and a calling upon my life. As my faith in God matured, I felt Him giving me greater clarity for the vision that was developing. There was a clear purpose and a hope: I was to help others suffering with mental illness, but didn't know yet how I was meant to get there. In some apparent confirmation of this, I was accepted into lay ministry training.

As certain areas of my life improved, demonic manifestations began to intensify again in our home. My childhood fear had never gone, and it seemed as if I was never going to be able to escape. Despite my faith and my involvement in church ministry, we continued to suffer. I knew it all stemmed from my childhood and the fear this had instilled in me, but as the attacks persisted night after night, the constant fear in my heart was getting the better of me. I simply couldn't go on like this anymore and I didn't know how to resolve it.

"Nicholas! Come back to bed!" my voice shook. To my amazement, my small six-year-old son about-turned on the stairs and started to walk back up them in silence. He was still asleep. I guided him into our own bed and waited until he had settled beside Paul before going to check on Jonathon. The air was still heavy.

Jonathon lay blissfully asleep on the top bunk in their bedroom as I crept into the bottom bunk to stay and protect our youngest child. The atmosphere in this room was particularly icy, stagnant, terribly wrong, and, as I lay down, I became aware of a black figure standing at the end of the bunk bed. I wanted to run back to Paul but it would mean running past the figure to do so and I didn't want to leave Jonathon alone with it. I lay there staring at it for what seemed hour upon hour, terrified and not daring to shut my eyes to sleep.

My eyes must have closed because suddenly I was being picked up and thrown across the room with an almighty force, crashing into the children's chest of drawers on the other side of the room. In pain and shock I opened my eyes. I was still in Nicholas's bed and the figure was still watching me. It was a dream, although there was no relief in knowing it because I had experienced it and felt the pain as if it had really happened—and the figure was still there watching me as if he had orchestrated it within my dreams. As I came to, I could hear sounds coming from my own bedroom. I knew I had to get to them, as Nicholas would be frightened by it.

The cries continued until Jonathon awoke from the noise as well and came tumbling down the ladder towards me. He saw the black figure too and screamed. Grabbing him, I made a dash past the figure and through the doorway, leaping into the bed beside the other two. Paul and Nicholas were both sitting bolt upright, visibly shaken by the noises going on in our own bedroom. The four of us sat huddled together with the light on for the rest of the night, Paul and I trying our best to reassure the boys, and failing miserably.

Amazingly, this was all very quickly and easily resolved when we attended a Freedom in Christ conference at our church with Neil Anderson. Both Paul and I went through the Steps to Freedom with a couple from Neil's US team. The ministry taught us about our authority in Christ as well as our true identity as children of God. This was a life-changing revelation, all open doors to the enemy were closed and once I knew that I had the authority to keep them closed, all demonic activity simply and easily ceased. This was the answer I had been looking for, and I later went on to work with Freedom in Christ and Steve Goss when he opened the first UK office.

My own vision for a residential ministry centre was becoming clearer, and we took our first steps towards this as we took in the first of three young women into our own home, each with severe difficulties with eating disorders and self-harm and helped them to walk in freedom themselves as we walked alongside them. I had not only changed my own thinking patterns to be more in line with the truth of who I was as a child of God, but I was now showing others.

Learning how to walk in freedom on a daily basis by challenging a faulty belief system, changing an ingrained pattern of behaviour, and renewing your mind, requires making the right choices on a daily basis. When life has been extremely traumatic, this is not something that you can simply do on your own overnight. I knew how long I had worked at this, and I knew that others would need proper facilities and a programme in place to help them get there. This became my prayer and my mission.

Chapter 14

The Prince of Peace

WE HAVE A GENTLE, compassionate, and loving God and He never raises the bar so high that we can't get over it. I did have to remove various blockages in order to receive the fullness of His healing, but they weren't as hard as I thought they would be, and the very thing that God wanted me to do was so simple and easy, but I'd missed it completely.

Other than myself and Richard, nobody else knew of Evie's existence because I fought to keep the DID hidden from everybody. After eight years of talking things through with Richard, however, whatever was keeping the story buried was as strong as ever and we were no nearer resolving it or understanding it.

In the midst of this journey, another family member was imprisoned for historical child abuse, which was shocking, and yet not shocking at the same time. The family had always known and, like a cat dragging a bedraggled captured bird through the cat flap to drop at your feet, so this relative frequently turned up with very young boys that the family turned a blind eye to. I'd often wondered as a child myself if the parents knew where their sons were, whether the boys had had to lie to say they were staying with friends, or if they were orphaned, or runaways, because who would let their child go on holiday with a grown man? Where did they keep coming from? There seemed to be such a multitude of questions that had never been voiced between the family, certainly not in front of me. Was it too much to bear, too much for a child to observe this obvious abusive behaviour, knowing that nobody was willing to intervene and help? It was another confusing strand running parallel in my childhood that I couldn't understand then and still can't understand now. I often wondered whether there was any significance to this and what else was buried in our family. There were so many unanswered questions to contend with.

I saw Nothing standing before me in my mind, and somehow outside of my mind, sullen and hauntingly desperate-looking, as usual. I reached out to her, saying, "Nothing, come to me; we can do this together. I can help carry this for you." This time Nothing came so close that her face seemed to melt into mine. I began falling backwards, slipping away into the depths of my mind like falling down a tunnel, and instinctively I knew that I was about to see something of what she was carrying.

But the feeling came before anything else. An overwhelming feeling of being so unbelievably bad again. The sensation was so strong that I felt crushed by it and my mind began racing and panicking to think what on earth I'd done that could possibly be as bad as this feeling implied I was.

I thought about the time I'd pulled my sister up the stairs by her hair in a fit of temper. That was bad and it was something that was upsetting to recall, but it still didn't equate to this overwhelming sense of something far worse. I wanted to argue with it, to scream at the feeling that I couldn't possibly be that bad, but I wanted to hear what the parts had to say, and to understand.

What followed was the appalling revelation that somebody had been hurt. I tried to stay calm as I allowed this part the freedom to get in touch with what was burdening her and to share it with me. The pictures began to surface in snippets.

I could see her running through grass, desperately trying to outrun someone she needed to escape from, tripping and falling on her face, the damp grass in her face as the hands reached out for her. The following scene unfolded within me like a film being shown within my mind: I saw a table covered in blood. I felt intense shock and disgust as I observed the scene. I couldn't tell where all the blood was coming from but could see that something had been cut up and strung up, or ripped apart. I could see a child being held there and forced to watch the ritual that was being performed. I was aware that she'd been crying and I could hear the screams in my mind that sounded as if they had somehow faded into the deepest place within me and got lost there. Her tears were felt as dried upon my face, but somehow I knew they were there. She was paralysed, utterly and completely traumatized by what was unfolding before her. I could see all the blood, but I couldn't tell if it was animal or human, but it seemed part of a ritual being performed by someone whose face I couldn't see. There were people around me but I couldn't see any of the faces, but I knew that my dad was there somewhere. I could hear a child's voice within me, insisting repeatedly, "It's not daddy's fault, he didn't know this was going to happen. This is a mistake, daddy didn't know this was going to happen. It's not daddy's fault."

I felt sickened by the scene before me and as I looked on, a whole range of other emotions and memories seemed to drop down like pegs into holes where they suddenly fitted where they never had before; things that had never made sense, now did. With the realization that this vision looked likely to be at the root of my past I also felt that I'd witnessed enough, and I couldn't bear to see or know anymore. I prayed, "Lord, please don't let it be this, please not this. I can't bear to see anymore, please make it stop and go away."

The scene faded in an instant, but finally one of the parts had shared something of her inner world and the horror she was carrying on my behalf to protect me. What more she carried I was yet to discover, if I could bear to allow it to surface into consciousness.

By chance, I came across a section in a book about a female survivor of satanic ritual abuse. She described various memories along with a ritual in which her legs had been cut off. A priest had remarked on the fact that she still clearly had two legs. The woman replied, "I know, and I can't see the join." The woman still believed that her legs had been amputated and the article posed the question as to whether this was the effect of hypnosis and drugs, or false memory syndrome. (Perry, 1996, p.79)

It was a strikingly similar account to one that I remembered as a 14-year-old and raised even more questions now about its meaning. How could two completely unrelated people have exactly the same bizarre experience? What could it possibly mean?

Whilst my mind could show me pictures that demonstrated an interpretation of the horror I had experienced, I also knew that they may not necessarily be accurate interpretations of what had in fact happened. Whatever happened may carry the same feelings, the same pain, but not necessarily the same visual interpretation, so I had to hold any visual 'memories' lightly, although this added to the overall sense of confusion.

There were so many difficult questions that simply couldn't be answered. I knew that I desperately needed more healing because Evie's persistent crying for mummy, which would be accompanied by overwhelming feelings of hopelessness and despair, was unbearable. I went along to a healing conference led by Chris Gore, the Director of Healing Ministries at Bethel Church in Redding, California. Over three days, Chris spoke about God's peace and healing in a way that I had never heard before. I was at breaking point, desperate for Evie to stop crying for mummy all the time and for integration. I had also developed some major problems with my hips and was struggling with having multiple surgeries and chronic pain. The part called Nothing seemed to be connected to the fear of doctors, as each time I went into hospital I was triggered and Nothing would switch in and run away.

Repeatedly I found myself in A&E after Nothing had tried to commit suicide. I knew that Nothing was therefore a suicidal part of me, connected to abuse and the fear of doctors, but I had no control over her switching and taking control after hospital or doctor's appointments. My life was unpredictable and out of control and I desperately needed healing and peace.

At the end of one of the morning sessions I approached Chris and asked him if he would pray for me. He asked me what I needed prayer for and as I gave him a quick explanation of the DID and my fear of doctors, his face fell! He would later admit to feelings of doubt and apprehension, but he laid hands on me and prayed. He prayed for the DID to be completely healed, for wholeness and unity as God intended, and that I would be filled with His shalom peace. He thanked God for His healing and told me to start thanking God for the healing before I stepped into it, from that moment on. Our brief meeting on that day was to change the course of my life completely, and maybe even his a little too!

I was filled with excitement over this completely new way of thinking about healing. God is outside of time, it is his desire to heal, and He has already given His peace and everything we need to walk in freedom. We can *choose* to receive it and step into that peace—*now*.

I didn't feel anything whatsoever when Chris prayed, but gradually a deep sense of His indescribable peace, beyond anything I'd ever known, seemed to settle in over me and remain with me, although there was no obvious healing at that point. Despite this, I continuously thanked God for healing me. Evie, meanwhile, continued to cry out for mummy but then two days later, as I lay in bed, I had a picture of her coming into the arms of Jesus and a strange electric shock-type jolt went through my head before I fell asleep. When I awoke the following morning, I was so full of peace and knew immediately that there had been a huge internal shift. I smiled constantly and felt as if I was glowing. There was complete silence in my mind for the first time in twelve years and I knew that I had found healing at last.

Nicholas, who had been suffering with crippling social anxiety, panic attacks, and suicidal thoughts himself, agreed to meet me three days later so that I could pray for him. We stood on the street during a busy lunch hour near London Bridge, as I prayed for him as Chris had taught us. Nicholas was completely healed on the spot! After years of panic attacks and social anxiety, it was lifted off in an instant, praise God! That same week, I prayed for somebody with infertility problems who conceived very soon afterwards and went on to have a daughter. Not only had I experienced healing, there had been an impartation and others around me were being healed as well.

Changing negative and destructive thought patterns is firstly all about choice, secondly about knowing the Prince of Peace, and thirdly choosing to live within that peace and healing—keeping our eyes fixed on Jesus, regardless of all else.

Chapter 15

Staying in a Place of Peace

EVERY PART OF ME knew truth and the Holy Spirit filled every part of my being. Of course, He always had done, but I had been fragmented and the child parts within me related and understood as children. For years I'd lived with the terrible uncertainty behind the meaning of Evie's persistent voice, and Nothing's desire to die, but I trusted God and He was encouraging me to trust Him and to wait. Some time later, I found this note from those early days, written in my journal:

> *What is this feeling—not emptiness, nor dissociation, or depression; no voices, internal or external. But I feel so tantalisingly close to being lured in towards dissociation, but I have to maintain control or the integration could break down and the parts become fragmented isolated islands within myself again. Whilst I'm hanging on, pulling all the threads together to stay whole, it feels spongy. Like osmosis, slipping in and out of a flimsy world, between unconscious and conscious. Held together by a fragile nest; my silver cage holds us all in.*
>
> *Yes, I think about you, Richard, but I am my own therapist now. I can choose whether to hold it together, or whether I'm going to let go. And even if I choose to let go, God will still be holding me in His hands. He will hold me until I can hold myself again. He is a patient and compassionate God. He will wait while I take time out. But I know that it won't achieve anything except to put everything on hold for a bit. Then I'll start again. But I can choose.*

The enemy knows our weaknesses and will always use them to tempt us. We also always have our default position to fall back on if we choose to. Our default position is the place that has become familiar and remains easy to slip back to, tempting at times when we want to relinquish responsibility. That's when the enemy steps in, and says "Go on then, you know you like it. . ." He would be just as quick to then accuse you of being useless and that you'd never been free, that the healing had never been true, and to snatch it away from you.

I knew that I had the choice; we all have the choice to walk in freedom and peace or to turn away. I knew how hard it was to make that choice when your mind is fragmented, and I had prayed earnestly from the beginning for an understanding that would help others.

I had experienced a miraculous healing, and others were being healed, but some were not. It felt as if there was still something missing. Something was missing in what I knew about my own past, as well as missing in how we approached this problem. I felt God saying that whilst I didn't know, He did, and could be trusted to lead the way.

> *He reveals deep and hidden things; he knows what lies in darkness, and light dwells with him. Daniel 2:22*

If we trust Him with the deep and hidden parts of ourselves, then we don't need to know everything and can let go. We know that the Bible is the beautiful inspired word of God and, even more than that, that the words are the very essence of God Himself. We can trust Him to hold us in His hands for all our lives whether in the midst of terrible suffering or at peace. Our suffering, however great, is nothing in comparison to the suffering that Jesus endured for us to be free, and we need always to keep that in perspective.

I discovered that when I learnt to keep my eyes on this, I experienced renewed strength to endure, as His word says in Hebrews 12:1–3 and I claimed it over my life. I turned truth around into statements that spoke life over me:

> 'Thank you, Lord, for dying for me, for all that You have accomplished for me, so I will not grow weary or weak.'

He has given us a plan for life, and no matter how complex or messy the circumstances or the past, His word works. If we have the mind of Christ, we can therefore listen to His voice, and allow Him to take us forwards in a partnership where we are not striving on our own to work things out. The answer is we don't always know the answers! We can't become frustrated in not knowing, because God will reveal what He chooses as and when He chooses and if He does not, then we trust Him anyway. Time is clearly not the same for God as it is for us and DID actually offers us a unique opportunity to understand this.

The fragmented child parts emerge in the present while still existing in the past as if the abuse is still happening. The fragmented parts still carry the same emotions and experiences as if they are still in that moment in the past because that is what they were created to do. Healing comes in the future, but to a child part that continues to exist in the past. Therefore, is God healing the adult in the future or reaching back into the past to heal the child right there at the moment she was hurting and needing to be rescued? In some way He does just this. The person suffering flashbacks experiences the past emotions in the present, but they are the consequences of past experiences. God was always there and does not choose to ignore us.

Imagine standing on the top of a tall building, looking down on a parade going past. From where you're looking down you can see the front and the rear of the parade all at once, but if you were on the ground you would only see the part of the parade passing by immediately in front of you. Let's imagine that the parade is our life. Most people experience their lives in the present: i.e., they see the parade as it passes by immediately in front of them from the pavement. We could describe this as a vertical experience of life. Most people experience their lives on a vertical level—only seeing what is passing by in the moment.

God, however, sees our life from above, as if He is standing on the top of the building looking down where He can see the front, the middle and the rear of the parade all at once. He has a horizontal view of the parade. This is an illustration of how God sees our lives: seeing the whole parade from the beginning to the end. We are not just existing in the present moment with God and He can reach in to any part of our lives in a moment and bring healing to either something in the past or the present, or all of it at once.

This illustration has continued to speak to me and I believe that people with DID also have a horizontal experience of their lives because the past continues to impact the present: the fragmented parts continue to experience the past trauma in the present. Instead of feeling frustrated with this experience of living, perhaps one can view it as the ability to experience your life as God sees your life. There is a depth of richness in this experience and the possibility to connect with emotions and experiences that would otherwise be lost to the person who experiences life vertically!

When a fragmented part, or 'alter,' switches in to take control, the person with co-conscious awareness will be aware of the emotions associated with that alter, although she will not be aware of the memories, the role or functions that that alter carried for her as a child. The adult host personality will feel the desire to run, for instance, but will have no understanding of what she needs to escape from, because she has no access to that information.

This can be a very painful and unsettling way of living, but there is some comfort, I think, in knowing that this horizontal experience of life is similar to the way God sees our lives. People who experience life vertically, who come into therapy in later life, may have difficulty accessing emotions linked to childhood events, but the person who experiences life horizontally has access to them all of the time! All of our experiences go in to creating the people we are today, and whether we develop vertically or horizontally, God sees all of what makes us who we are. The DID patient may feel as if life continues to feel threatening and painful because she experienced times that were indeed very threatening and painful, and the alters are still experiencing those emotions as if they are trapped in time. Those experiences have shaped the person that exists today, and whilst it may feel as if she is disadvantaged by her ongoing experience of threat and pain, it might be helpful to see it from a different perspective: you have the same horizontal experience of your life as God has of your life!

Rather than seeing it as a disability, perhaps it might be possible to view it as the gift God gave you to survive and to view it today as an enriched experience that does not, for one moment, change who you are as a child of God. It may seem hard to describe it as an enriched experience of life, but God wants us to take His perspective, to be dependent on Him, to know that He is always with us, that we are not alone and now safe under His protection. These compassionate responses need to be brought to the alters in order to convince the whole system that they are now safe.

I had been involved in ministry for a while when we took in three severely unwell young women into our family to care for them, by walking alongside them and showing them how to renew their minds and choose truth. I had been involved with Freedom in Christ Ministries since it came to the UK and was applying this repentance model to a daily walk with Him. I had been praying about a vision for a residential home for people with complex mental health problems long before I had even met my husband, Paul, and I continued to pray into this. I hadn't anticipated discovering that I had DID along the way.

Sometimes we can't understand what God is doing or where He is taking us when things are tough and sometimes it's not until much further down the line that we can look back and understand why. I could not understand at the time why I'd relapsed, but He brought me carefully and safely through, during which I experienced things that would change the direction of the vision but still brought us to the exact date we had known the next phase of the work would begin.

During the wait I gained experience that would be invaluable: several promotions led to a senior management role in the NHS, overseeing eight departments and about 70 people. I gained a good understanding of how the referral system worked from primary to secondary care, as this was one of the contracts I managed. Whilst this time was frustrating as I waited, I was also amazed at the speed of those promotions and knew that God was in each of them and they were part of His plan.

The date eventually came to leave the NHS. God made it very clear that this was the date I'd committed in my mind, and envisaged as the time, seven years earlier (when the children would both finish sixth form) as I was made redundant at exactly this point! I used my redundancy money to fund the start of an intense eight year period of clinical training as a psychotherapist.

Every door we pushed opened. A chance conversation with an old acquaintance led to the offer of a room within a building where we could start. Money started coming in and covered a year's rent before we'd even started. We were stunned to discover it was the very same building where I first received private psychiatric treatment after I met Paul— where I felt listened to for the first time. What's more, we ended up with the very same upstairs room where I had spent hours talking twenty years earlier. This seemed confirmation that this was where 'Still the Hunger' was meant to be because it aligned so perfectly with the vision of bridging the gap between church and mental health, with the provision of a new Christian therapeutic community where people would be listened to, receive psychotherapy, discipleship, and healing.

The room at 11 Glebe Road was symbolic of that bridge between church and mental health, of bringing God into that very room where it all started when I first began to learn to walk in freedom. Therapy and discipleship had been kept very much apart, and I had to bring it together myself. This added to the fragmented experience I struggled with. I knew how important it would be for others to have a different experience to the one I had had because I don't believe that God differentiates between physical, psychological, or spiritual healing. All three overlap and we should not treat them separately. We are each physical, emotional, and spiritual beings and we must treat from a more holistic perspective that includes all three.

The name came from Psalm 17:14 'you still the hunger of those you cherish' (NIV, 2000) because this felt to be the message God was conveying—that He sustains and satisfies every deep unmet need within us. It is to Him we must go for the emptiness that so many of us are trying to meet inappropriately and unsuccessfully. Here was a place from where we would lead people to a God Who could be depended on and trusted, Who could meet those deep desires for love and healing in those who only knew emptiness and pain. A place for those who had been trying unsuccessfully to meet those needs through food, self-harm, and any other dysfunctional methods. This is where the healing of damaged emotions would begin, where therapy met God, the Wonderful Counsellor.

Chapter 16

Stilling the Hunger in Others

NICHOLAS AND JONATHON, spent several days during their summer break from university one year visiting all the GP practices in the Reading area to talk to them and persuade them to display our posters and flyers in their waiting rooms.

I believed that the programme was to have a biblical foundation and that God was calling me to bridge the gap between mental health and the church, but I had no idea how this would work with non-Christians coming via GP practices, even though it felt right to take our message outside the church. If the message was based on knowing your identity and authority as a Christian and learning how to renew your mind with God's word, then what did we have to offer non-Christians if they didn't believe—and would it get us into trouble? Despite my apprehension, we stuck to the calling.

People started to come, until at one point we had an entire group of people who had come as non-Christians. As we practiced meeting people where they were, never forcing our faith on anyone, loving them and accepting them as Jesus would have done, each one accepted Christ as Lord and Saviour! Whilst this was a beautiful aspect of the work, we also provided professional clinical therapy in its own right for those not looking for faith. I am reminded of the passage in Luke 17:12–18 where God heals ten lepers and only one returns to give glory to God:

> *[12]As he entered one village, ten men approached him, but they kept their distance, for they were lepers. [13]They shouted to him, "Mighty Lord, our wonderful Master! Won't you have mercy on us and heal us?" [14]When Jesus stopped to look at them, he spoke these words: "Go to be examined by the Jewish priests." They set off, and they were healed while walking along the way. [15]One of them, a foreigner from Samaria, when he discovered that he was completely healed, turned back to find Jesus, shouting out joyous praises and glorifying God. [16]When he found Jesus, he fell down at his feet and thanked him over and over, saying to him, "You are the Messiah." This man was a Samaritan. [17]"So where are the other nine?" Jesus asked. "Weren't there ten who were healed? [18]They all refused to return to give thanks and give glory to God except you, a foreigner from Samaria?" (TPT)*

This is Jack's story. At his assessment, Jack told me that he had been suspended previously at an NHS therapeutic community and told firmly that if he wanted help, then he had to conform. He said that he felt that this meant that he could not express himself properly and talked about his aggressive and violent history which had landed him in trouble many times. I explained to Jack that I felt that it was possible to express himself without being aggressive and, despite his reservations about this, he agreed to come and try.

Stilling the Hunger in Others

As I was unsure about whether he would be a disruptive influence, or be threatening towards others on the programme, and have little respect for the building and contents when in a violent rage, I arranged for plenty of prayer cover during those first days, as I had no idea what to expect. The Jack we subsequently met was considerate of others and extremely funny, even if his use of language was rather colourful at times.

For some time he avoided the worship and discipleship sessions on a Friday afternoon, but as he began to hear how much others were getting from the sessions, he decided to stay as well, although he made it very clear that he would not be lured into the 'sandals and tambourines' brigade!

Jack sat quietly next to me during his first worship session without singing, and then left for the weekend. On Monday morning, he announced that he would not sit next to me again if he stayed for the worship session, and when asked why, he said that he could feel God radiating off me. I suggested to him that maybe he was experiencing God for himself! Jack went quiet as he thought about this and then said that he felt strange.

It became apparent that Jack was experiencing the Holy Spirit coming in waves upon him during the group therapy session. He had never even heard of the Holy Spirit before! Over the course of several subsequent group therapy sessions Jack would be glued to his chair, with his feet stuck firmly to the floor, and tears streaming down his cheeks as he experienced these 'whooshes' as he described them each time I spoke any scriptural truth within the group discussions, even when he didn't know the words weren't just part of normal therapy and conversation.

Jack wrote the following account of what he experienced:

> 'I was sitting in the group and we were talking about what was going on for us. I began to feel His presence, or the Holy Spirit, as Bev calls Him. As she spoke, He slowly came into me, followed by a sensation of waves surging through me, like electric currents, which gradually became more and more powerful. I think I was trying not to resist it whilst also trying to manage it, but gradually the power was getting greater and greater. It was such a nice feeling that I didn't want it to stop. I was aware that a force was firmly rooting my feet to the ground. Tears were streaming down my face. Why? I wasn't upset or angry, but I felt

very emotional. The waves alternated in strength, sometimes stronger, sometimes weaker, but never left me.

Then I was on the front row of a plane, with Jesus as the co-pilot. He came out to see me and seemed to know that I was petrified. He didn't say anything, but He knew everything about me. Whilst He said nothing, I also heard Him say, "Come with me on the most exciting, brilliant, wonderful, awesome journey of your life."

I am still on the plane. I can feel my legs are still crossed, fighting to stay rooted to the ground. I am not scared, although I can feel myself shaking. I have this sense of being on an unbelievable journey to somewhere where only good is going to happen. I am aware of the others in the group and want to give one of the others my hand to give them also a zap of the power I can feel in me to help them. I feel I need to come back to the group but then more whooshes come in.

Whoosh! I think this is what Bev would say is the Holy Spirit, but like doubting Thomas I want to say, "Prove it." I don't know what it is and I can only try to describe it, if that's even possible.

I felt I was being invited by Jesus to travel with Him. He knows me. He is holding out His hand to me and saying, "Come with me, and look at you soaring high in the sky! You can be great when you fly with me."

I believe, and I am willing to take His hand and trust the person leading me. I feel myself take that leap of faith. I am ready, or at least to take a first step, towards having a relationship with Jesus. I feel at peace and, for the people who know me, that is something I have never had, but crave down to my bones. I have tears in my eyes now, a cup of tea in my hands. I have been blessed. I well up. I am not cured yet and I know that I have a long way to go, but I am at least on the right track.'

This particular event occurred just before Easter in a normal group therapy session, not a worship or discipleship session. During that same group session, Sally told us that she could see Jesus standing behind Jack, looking straight at her and reaching out His hand towards her. He was asking her to come to Him too, and telling her that everything would be okay. At the same time as this, Jolene asked me what was making a

Stilling the Hunger in Others

card on the mantelpiece glow, asking whether I was knocking the mantelpiece somehow because the card kept moving. We turned to look but couldn't see what Jolene was seeing; she could see a bright light shining onto the image of the Passover supper on the Easter card, but the light wasn't coming from anywhere in the room. Neither was my chair knocking the mantelpiece and there was no drought in the room. We gave the card to Jolene to take home to keep, much to her delight, and she also asked Jesus into her life!

When Margaret first made contact, she asked me over the phone if she had to believe in God to come because she was a Buddhist. I reassured her that she didn't, but that the programme had a Christian foundation, which she decided she felt okay about. The other members of the group were attending the Freedom in Christ discipleship course that we were running and had just had their corporate Steps Day. The group were enthusing about this and the difference it had made to them. They were talking between themselves about how to challenge negative thinking patterns and how to identify and deal with strongholds.

Margaret had some experience with CBT (cognitive behaviour therapy) and so understood what they were talking about in these terms. It was during her third week that Margaret took us by surprise when she came to the group with some homework she had been doing on her own to challenge her negative thoughts—with God's Word. Margaret asked Jesus into her life.

Six months after my own healing we went as a family to Bethel to see Chris and visit the Healing Rooms. Chris came out to meet us in the foyer at Bethel and took the four of us straight round to where the team were praying and worshipping before starting. I was overwhelmed by the number of people in this room preparing for prayer ministry with the people who were queuing up outside for healing. As we stood and watched, Chris walked into the centre of the huge packed room of people and started to say, "Do you remember the lady I've been telling you about who was healed when I visited the UK? Well, here she is!" Chris then took me by the hand and led me into the centre of the group, gave me the microphone and told me to give my testimony! People were clapping and crying, and during the course of the morning several people came up to tell me how they had been following my story with Chris since he had returned. I had no idea that Chris was passing on my messages to everybody else, and that my story was being told all over the world and people were being healed just from hearing it!

Chris has his version of the moment he prayed for me and what subsequently happened is recorded in his message, 'The Spirit that Destroys Chaos,' which is available to purchase from the Bethel online store. While we were visiting, the Bethel team filmed an interview between Chris and me that I was able to then share with our clients back at Still the Hunger, along with the talk The Spirit that Destroys Chaos. We have remained friends ever since, and the story is available on YouTube from churches all over the world.

Whilst there was exciting progress at Still the Hunger and in my emotional health, my physical health deteriorated and I continued to undergo regular surgery on my hips and spine. I also continued to struggle with doctors and it was after yet another operation on my hips that it became apparent that not all the alters had fused, and going into hospital was still triggering. The realisation that still more healing was needed was a massive blow. Emotionally low, I also felt like a fraud, with the same compulsive need to keep something a secret, which felt like a massive burden.

I had been seeing Professor David Veale at the North London Priory prior to the healing I experienced when Chris prayed for me. David had supported me through the cycle of surgery and fear of doctors, eventually enabling me to disclose the sexual abuse that had taken place at the hospital over 25 years earlier, of which I had never told anybody. With his help, I reported it to the police as well as to the GMC and to the hospital where it had occurred. The hospital supported me and also reported him to the GMC.

This was all going on throughout my clinical training. Alongside the clinical work in London, I was also managing the therapeutic community programme at Still the Hunger, whilst going in and out of hospital for surgery and managing chronic pain. Despite years of intense study and personal therapy, I still didn't know why I had developed DID, but I knew that I was still hurting—my body was giving me very clear messages of that. Every part of who I was, both physically and spiritually, was crying out in pain, protesting at how hard it was to continue to hide this secret within me. As I studied and worked with repetitive cycles of behaviour in others, I began to notice my own tendency with secrets, which led to the realisation that there was still a massive secret being held within me that was continuously being re-enacted through the physical pain I was experiencing.

I continued to manage the intense raw emotions that surfaced due to the way they had been fragmented; I continued to bring every thought and behaviour in line with truth. I continued to speak healing and peace over myself, and thanked God for His healing and I knew that He would complete the good work begun in me. I continued to lead others to Jesus, to walk alongside them on their own recovery journey, continued to pray for others to be healed, continued to teach, and continued working in absolute faith that God's timing is always perfect and that He can be trusted.

I read extensively on trauma and DID. It seemed that God was sending us people with a wide range of problems, but frequently those with the most complex presentations. I saw that DID had many different manifestations. Within the material that I read I came across EMDR (Eye Movement Desensitisation Reprocessing) as being a useful treatment modality for trauma, BDD and DID and I decided to try it to address my fear of doctors. I went to see a psychologist who offered EMDR, and within two months my problem with doctors had improved dramatically.

EMDR seems to enable the processing of memories and trauma through eye movements, which releases information held within the central nervous system and the amygdala (where it is experienced in present tense), and moves it into the hippocampus as it's processed and filed away in the past. As the information is released and processed, flashbacks will cease. EMDR enabled the fear of doctors to be processed and for the part, Nothing, who was associated with this fear of doctors, to therefore integrate and fuse, at last. The emotions associated with doctors were simply and quickly processed and healed.

God uses a variety of tools to bring about emotional, physical, and spiritual healing, including not only the understanding of God's word to renew your mind, but also clinical tools such as EMDR, alongside prayer ministry and deliverance. We have seen amazing examples of God healing through the processing of memories through talking directly to the client and bringing peace, revelation, and transformation into past situations.

The processing of trauma during EMDR results in the desensitisation of the memory. The brain processes stored information from visual memory, sound, emotions, smell, and physical memory, until they can be stored away in the past without causing further flashbacks of sensory symptoms. Sometimes the memory itself will fade or it will be transformed into something more positive that enables the person to move on. Sometimes a person is unaware of how it has actually changed, but they discover the problem is no longer a trigger.

It is important to state that EMDR does not cause false-memory syndrome and it is not a form of hypnosis: the eye movements are thought to trigger a response that may be related to REM sleep and seem to enable material that is held within the amygdala (where it continues to be triggered by present-day stimuli), to surface to conscious recall and pass quickly to the hippocampus. As it does so, the brain not only brings to recall the negative experiences but also a variety of positive memories. The positive memories seem to bring a healthier balance and remain within conscious recall, whereas the negative memories fade.

Once I completed my training as a psychodynamic psychotherapist after 7 years, I went on to qualify as an EMDR therapist a year later.

Chapter 17

Integrating Therapy, Healing, and Discipleship

Invitation to the Thirsty

[1] "Come, all you who are thirsty, come to the waters; and you who have no money, come, buy and eat! Come, buy wine and milk without money and without cost. [2] Why spend money on what is not bread, and your labour on what does not satisfy? Listen, listen to me, and eat what is good, and you will delight in the richest of fare. [3] Give ear and come to me; listen, that you may live. [12] You will go out in joy and be led forth in peace."

Isaiah 55:1–3,12 (NIV)

SYSTEMATICALLY ABUSED and traumatised children often behave in such a way that continues to get them into trouble as they unconsciously re-enact patterns related to aspects of their experiences from the past. Others may feel exasperated by the situations they seem to get into and may give up on them, but the situation may not be as it appears to those on the outside. If someone has learnt to split off, or block out, traumatic and unpleasant experiences or feelings, then it's likely that if some other unpleasant situation arises, that she will comply or adapt to the situation in the way she learnt to as a child. With DID, parts may automatically switch in to manage a situation that evokes similar feelings, whilst another part may actually have no explanation for why they keep getting into the same situations, or how to change.

This is where I found myself during the early part of my recovery when my church was first trying to help me as a young Christian: somehow back in a situation where I was surrounded by all the support I could need in one part of my life, but being groomed and abused in another, and not a soul knew about it. Instead, I began behaving in the way I had before—the old coping mechanisms I was familiar with: self-harm, through which I could direct all the disgust and hate onto myself, as before.

Sadly, the church didn't have the experience to know what was happening without me being able to say anything, and suggested I prayed harder. I was praying really, really, hard, but I was getting depressed by the unconscious and conscious feelings of isolation and the automatic conditioned response to bury the abuse. This confusing scenario put me in a very familiar situation where doctors were caregivers, colleagues, and authority figures, as well as abusers. I gradually discovered various triggering factors linked to all the feelings from my childhood with parents who terrified the living daylights out of me, who were meant to love me but also didn't seem to care one ounce about me. As a new Christian, it now felt as if the church were also playing into the same familiar roles where those I loved saw me as a bad Christian because it looked as if I'd gone back to my old patterns of behaviour and wasn't trusting God. I was fighting the old patterns of control, denial, and disgust, and turning these feelings upon myself, which was another learnt pattern of behaviour in order to keep those I loved in a good place in my mind. It was safer to believe that I was the one who was bad and that everyone was right—this was the way it had always been.

Integrating Therapy, Healing, and Discipleship

I was, however, taught how to claim the truth that God would not leave me like this—He would complete the good work He had begun in me. I claimed this over my life every day, along with other statements, such as He had not given me a spirit of fear, but of power, love and a sound mind, and that nothing was too difficult for Him. I knew I'd get there.

I can vividly remember sitting on the stairs as a 10-year-old, thinking how much I wanted to run away, but not knowing what I was running from. This feeling stayed with me throughout my adult life, and I came to realise that it belonged to another part of me that was holding memories to which I had no access.

As with any therapist in training, I had to be in intensive personal therapy myself, where I continued to have to juggle my faith alongside therapy, the two always kept separate. It was okay for me to talk about my faith but never to work on it together or to pray together, which would have been frowned upon. So, I had to do it for myself. I chose to do a rigorous clinical training, rather than Christian counselling, because I wanted that depth of clinical theory to draw upon for the work I felt God calling me to.

For the fragmented Christian, however, offering a clinical technique in isolation is yet another fragmented experience to contend with. I believe it's so important to see each person as more than somebody who is suffering with an emotional problem, because we are all physical, emotional, and spiritual beings. All these aspects of life need integrating and treating together because I don't believe God sees people like this— I believe He sees hurting people. Who's to say that somebody who is experiencing a physical health problem is not doing so as a consequence of a spiritual problem, something that has been born out of anger, jealousy, bitterness, or unforgiveness, for example, that has been held within the body and mind, or the central nervous system, of somebody for so many years. This pain has to find expression at some point, in some way. Physical symptoms begin to manifest—are they psychosomatic or are they real? Even if they are real, like eczema that needs a topical lotion to be applied, or IBS that responds better to a change of diet, it is well-known to psychotherapists that these, and so many other conditions, can be caused by emotional issues and stress.

We must not forget the spiritual aspects of both physical and emotional well-being, of course.

Chapter 18

Faulty Perspectives

I KNEW THERE HAD always been a problem with the way I had perceived myself. God has given us clear guidelines for living healthily. If we live outside of His framework, then we allow Satan ground in our lives, which could result in not only internal emotional torment, but the bitterness and anger that we harbour within ourselves can be forced out into a physical manifestation of the internal pain we don't verbalise in a healthy way. For example, a person may suffer with a heart condition as a consequence of repressed rage. It is well-known that those who suffer with anger are more likely to also suffer with their hearts.

I discovered the importance and value of good therapy, but the difficulty caused by having to maintain a boundary between therapy and faith. The two have to come together. For those nearer the beginning of their faith journey it's very hard to know how to renew your mind and take authority over thoughts and feelings on your own. I knew that this was what God was putting on my heart: the importance of the provision of a clinical model where psychotherapy, discipleship, and healing would be an integrated experience to bring about whole healing.

This combination is crucial for those who are so damaged. It's so important to be able to process past experiences, to find a voice, find the words, to be heard and understood, but to also discover another perspective—and to see that it wasn't your fault. Whatever happened wasn't because you were worthless, useless, and not good enough, but that this was the immature child's brain's perspective of the situation at the time. People may need help to see how the choices made were born out of negative experiences, but that they can be undone and turned around because nobody is so far gone as to be beyond the redemptive power of Jesus.

All of this takes time as we learn how to walk in freedom. You may already be free in Christ, as it says in Galatians 5:1, but you have to learn how to walk in that freedom. We need to become familiar with sitting at the seat of the table God has prepared for us: a table that is laid out with a feast of abundance where He longs to sit and spend time with you. A seat where you learn who you are in Christ, how precious and loved you are: where you learn about your authority in Christ and how to renew your mind with truth.

For those who are so deeply damaged and have developed dysfunctional patterns of behaviour that are ingrained, they can't simply do that on their own without somebody walking alongside them in the form of not only a Christian mentor, but also an experienced therapist. We need to equip the church to help bring this together because the NHS is so tied by ethical boundaries and time-limited therapy due to the constraints of funding and risk. Equally, the church does not have to operate as an isolated island and try to manage every one of its flock alone; the church can fill the gap that exists between the NHS and the church, but only if it makes use of experienced clinicians in a collaborative capacity and learns that it can work together with others.

As for the rest of my own healing, it's been a long journey with the pieces coming together through all these things: psychotherapy, EMDR, discipleship, and prayer. I knew enough when the DID emerged that this meant what I thought I knew about my childhood was not as it appeared or I wouldn't have DID, because I knew that DID occurs in very young children who are extremely traumatised. The very young child's brain learns how to fragment off the unbearable experiences and emotions into other parts of the mind so that the child can continue to function in other areas of her life, such as in school.

I knew that my childhood had been terrifying, but as the DID developed, I learnt that it was so much worse than I'd thought. My psychotherapy with Richard helped me to begin to process the top layers that I actually remembered, but I seriously battled with who I could trust with the DID. I had a lot of help from Professor David Veale, who taught me Compassion-focused Therapy (CfT), which I've also integrated into my clinical work with others, as I discovered the huge benefits of this. I am enormously grateful for the input that he gave me during extremely difficult times. He teaches compassion, and he certainly demonstrated enormous compassion towards me as he listened patiently, while I tried to make sense of what had happened to me, whilst continuing to trust me as a developing trainee psychotherapist. I have also had the support of an excellent GP, and, whilst it took some time to convince me, the consultants who have helped me with my orthopaedic problems, have shown me that doctors can indeed be professional and trusted.

My healing came in several stages, with the biggest change occurring after Chris Gore prayed for me. His teaching on choosing how to stay in a place of peace, and how to keep your eyes on Jesus instead of on negative distractions, including sickness, was transformative. His teaching on thanking God for His healing and His peace before experiencing it as a step of faith, has not only had a huge impact upon my life, but also on the lives of those we support at Still the Hunger. So many people see peace as something that they long to feel, and pray for that *feeling*, and whilst it's great to feel it, peace is not a feeling as we imagine—it's something more akin to faith in Christ in many respects. It trivialises peace to imagine it as simply a pleasant feeling that comes and goes; it is so much more complex and wonderful than that. We can choose to stay in a place of peace by keeping our eyes fixed on Jesus, rather than on our own circumstances, and stepping into each day from this perspective changes everything. In John 14:27, Jesus says:

> *"I leave the gift of peace with you—my peace. Not the kind of fragile peace given by the world, but my perfect peace. Don't yield to fear or be troubled in your hearts—instead, be courageous!"*

Learning to love myself through the compassion work taught me by David Veale has been absolutely crucial to walking in freedom, but EMDR has also brought about not only the healing of my fear of doctors, but also finally brought about the recovery of my past at long last, and the final integration and fusion of the fragmented parts of my mind when I used it in conjunction with prayer. I had no specialised therapy for DID, as I could never access funding for this and no private therapists would undertake such a work, even though I was working with several clients with DID myself. As with all of my recovery, I was to do it myself, in partnership with God. Occasionally, I would enlist the help of a dear friend, a Christian counselling psychologist who also had some experience with EMDR, and I studied DID extensively alongside the rest of my training.

For several years, I had suffered with strange flashbacks and nightmares. I saw snippets of scenes that I couldn't fit in anywhere to the story I thought was my life, which I knew had gaps in it. I occasionally suffered with physical sensations where I would re-live experiences as 'body memories,' without any visual memory or recollection of what it was about. These were terrifying experiences. Several times I experienced the sensation of choking and feeling like I was being strangled, and a terrified child part would start crying that she couldn't breathe and was going to die—in front of Paul and the boys, who'd never seen anything like it before. Other times I would be on my knees crying with pain that felt as if I had just been raped, whilst having no memory of ever being raped. As a family we prayed together as much as we could, while I continued to thank God for healing me and working constantly on renewing my mind.

For a little while the DID seemed to come and go—I would have six months free and then there was a trigger and it would re-emerge again for a period. More healing followed, another trigger, etc., which was frustrating, but I've discovered that healing from DID can be a bit like that and comes in stages. God was still bringing about healing, nothing had gone wrong, it was just a complex process that needed more time and I was moving in the right direction. I had been healed, there had been huge progress and change, and I never wavered from thanking God for His healing.

Whilst I was battling with my own physical health, several of my team got sick: Rachel, who had worked alongside me since we opened, had a serious accident and suffered a brain injury, and three of the team died suddenly. "Why?" I kept asking God. Why all this pain, enormous sadness, and such a struggle, alongside seeing others being set free and lives being transformed? Obviously, this was a spiritual battle, we were treading on enemy territory, and God was making a new path through the desert of so many lives. But that gives Satan more power than he has, and this is a mistake.

We have to choose not to look at the problem because that causes us to take our eyes off Jesus—we have to keep our eyes fixed on Him and all that He has done for us and walk in freedom, not crawling along as a victim, but standing tall as a precious child of God who is already free!

We were seeing more people with complex needs and DID, and I was on a mission to see healing for those affected by trauma, child abuse, and chronic pain. The more I searched and prayed, the more I also discovered about my own past, and the more complicated and harrowing it seemed. The pain served only to bring me closer to God and help me to understand more of His heart.

I understood that as a child, my mind had made sense of the situation by deciding it was because I wasn't as pretty as my sister, and I believed she was loved more than me because she was smaller and fairer. So I grew up to hate the way I looked. I had always battled with body image, but whilst I didn't understand initially the unconscious reasons for this, I knew that God did. I also knew that He had created me, He knew every part of me, and He knew what had happened to me. He told me that whilst I didn't know how to solve it, He did, and He would put me, and others, back together again. I have always known that He would complete the good work He had begun in me.

In Colossians 1:17 it says:

> *He existed before anything was made, and now everything finds completion in him.* ^{20–22} *by the blood of his cross, everything in heaven and earth is brought back to himself – back to its original intent, restored to innocence again! Even though you were once distant from him, living in the shadows of your evil thoughts and actions, he reconnected you back to himself. He released his supernatural peace to you through the sacrifice of his own body as the sin-payment on your behalf so that you would dwell in his presence. And now there is nothing between you and God, for he sees you as holy, flawless, and restored. (TPT)*

I understood that the healing was happening in stages and in His perfect timing. Had He revealed all of it to me at the beginning, then I would never have coped with all of what was to come. His Word says that I will be restored, that nothing can come between me and Him that will prevent me from being holy and flawless. Nothing can prevent me from being reconnected and drawn back to Himself. If I was living in a place of peace and hope, then there had to be meaning behind my pain too. Instead of seeing it as constant enemy attack, which gives Satan more power than he has, I chose instead to listen to God and learn from it.

As I changed my perspective and learnt to go deeper and listen, I became aware of something on His heart and a message that He wanted me to bring. He told me that there are consequences to living your life while hating yourself. "You cannot expect there will not be consequences," He said. An example would be those who smoke—they end up with a cough, or worse. The same is true with self-hatred, however it manifests: living with an internal drive based on self-punishment born out of self-hatred and worthlessness is living in a place that is totally contradictory to the way God sees us. I felt God's enormous sadness over this as I prayed about my own physical pain and thought about all those years when I had not seen myself as He sees me. As I listened, He talked to me about how much He loves us and how much it hurts Him to see His children hurting themselves and living like this. He told me how He longs for us to see ourselves as He sees us, fearfully and wonderfully made, deeply loved, and part of His family, blessed with every spiritual blessing. If we could only see it the way He sees it, then we would live in peace with ourselves and we would see the terrible distraction these beliefs and behaviour patterns are, that ultimately lead us away from Him and the truth of who we are as His loved and special children.

We have a responsibility towards ourselves and there are consequences when we don't live according to God's framework, which has been set out for our own safety according to His love for us. It says in: Jeremiah 26:4–6:

> *"If you refuse to listen to me and live by my teaching that I've revealed so plainly to you, and if you continue to refuse to listen to my servants the prophets that I tirelessly keep on sending you. . .then I'll make this temple a pile of ruins like Shiloh, and I'll make this city nothing but a bad joke worldwide." (MSG)*

I believe that in these words, He could also be referring to the temple as our bodies, as the living temple—the place within which his Holy Spirit dwells within us. We are all aware of the physical toll from cigarettes, drink, drugs, and starvation, for example, but I believe the consequences of years of self-hatred will also find expression later in life and may do so in the form of chronic pain and disease. Our bodies cannot survive under the weight of such hatred, whether you want to consider that from a psychological perspective or a spiritual one. There are consequences. And I believe this causes God enormous sadness because He has so much love for us and it hurts Him to see so many of us hating ourselves and despising what He has created as fearfully and wonderfully made.

If we could only see ourselves as He sees us, then it would be impossible to get so caught up in self-hatred and all the things we do to ourselves. If we really understood the depth of His love for each one of us, and how special we are, then we would walk in the freedom He intends for us. I got a glimpse of His enormous grief over this and felt the burden He was putting on me to bring this teaching: start living as He sees you now and not as somebody who was ever flawed or permanently damaged by past experiences. To believe anything other than this is so not true. We are free now; we're not slaves to bondage, but free children of God, from the moment you ask Him into your life.

Burying emotions, whether the pain of abuse, anger, unforgiveness, anxiety, or trauma means it will have to find expression somehow eventually in our body. It has to come out somehow. Sometimes our brain learns to discharge it into physical symptoms as it did as a child if we never learnt to express emotions verbally. When we are born there is no distinction between emotional and physical distress for the developing baby—feelings of hunger, being wet, cold, hot, and feeling loved are all wrapped up in being fed, and love is a physical experience that connects us to mum, or the main caregiver. There is a merged experience with the baby not being able to distinguish between self and mum: with security, identity, feeling satisfied, warm, and loved all being found in being fed and held. As the brain develops, it learns to separate from mum, and begins to identify the difference between physical and emotional distress, but for those for whom there is a mismatch with mum or the main parental figure, for whatever reason, or they never learn to understand what is happening around them and find words for it, it may come out in physical symptoms in childhood, and this may become a learnt pattern in adulthood.

Self-hatred gets locked into your body and there are consequences, however you want to look at it. Whether you want to see this from a psychological perspective or a spiritual one—living outside of God's truth allows the enemy ground in your life. God wants us to stop living like this, and to help others to see how loved and special they are. We are physical, emotional, and spiritual beings, created to be connected with God, and with each other. There is no distinction between physical or emotional pain, or spiritual conflict. The answer is the same. Come close to Him, abide in Him, and get help to walk in freedom, but stop hurting yourself with self-hatred and self-harm, however you're doing it, because there are consequences to living like this.

I don't believe that this is something that should be heard as a threat or a curse upon your life. It feels to me as if God has said that this is a natural cause-and-effect outcome—if you live for years in a place of bitterness, anger, and self-hatred, you'll get ill. But everything can be reversed and put right, as His word says: everything finds completion in Him. No matter where you are, or where you have been, He has reconnected you back to Himself through Christ. He has released His peace to you through Him, and He sees you, and therefore you are holy, flawless, and restored. Washed clean.

If God says you are fearfully and wonderfully made, and so loved and precious to Him, but you're not living like a son or daughter of the King, then you're living outside of Him and exposed to the enemy. God loves to heal; it's His will and desire to heal. He is also the Wonderful Counsellor, and we can come to Him and talk about everything. For those who are severely damaged and hurting, it takes time and somebody to walk alongside them to keep pointing them back to truth for a while.

One of the things I began to discover at Still the Hunger was that clients seemed to find it easier to accept that God loved them than to love themselves. They have internalised the childhood bully or abuser, and they continue to play out this role towards themselves as their minds are trying to make sense of the original situations within which it occurred. They are re-enacting the abuse themselves and they continue to suffer— not from the original trauma, but at their own hands. It's hard to treat yourself with respect when nobody else has done, so people need to be shown how to do it by being shown that love and compassion by others first, and through our example, they get to see the love and compassion of God. Compassion-focused Therapy enables people to learn to redress this balance, but there's nothing clever about it, because God modelled it first! Through His word, and the examples of others, we can learn to undo past patterns of thinking and behaviour and be compassionate to ourselves as, after all, we also have the mind of Christ.

Walking free comes with creating a safe space within you, where all the fragmented, frightened parts feel safe enough to come back together— that's the same whether you're DID or not. All the parts, all the struggles and pain, need to know the love of Jesus being brought into them, because only He can reach back into the past and transform the memories and experiences we carry. Tools like EMDR, Compassion-focused Therapy, and other clinical models, all work effectively alongside renewing your mind and choosing to stay in a place of peace. We can do that with the support of others—by integrating love, as it's meant to be.

Chapter 19

Forty Years

THIS STORY HAS BEEN written out of the experiences I have had as I have learnt more about God and my relationship with Him, as I have learnt to walk in freedom and healing. As I have been walking in it and learning it for myself, I have been teaching it to others. Working in partnership with God has allowed us to witness amazing transformation and healing at Still the Hunger. We are all on a journey and we don't need to wait until everything is perfect before we begin helping others. God takes our brokenness and weakness and turns it into something beautiful, something that brings glory to Himself, not to us, and in our weakness we are strong.

If you have Christ in you, then regardless of what you have been through, or are going through, you have something in you that others may not have, and God can work through you, as He has through me, to bring hope to somebody else. With Christ in you, you have something to give, whatever your circumstances, so start walking in freedom now, not once everything is perfect. Focus on the achievements, the miracles, the progress. Write them down, remember them, and talk about them. Remind yourself and others of them. Speak them out! His Spirit is activated into the lives of others as we speak out what He has done in our lives, and people are healed just from hearing it.

It is forty years since I first asked Jesus into my life. It has been forty years of learning to listen to Him and learning to walk in freedom and trust Him. Forty years of processing what happened during my childhood and disentangling myself from it. I may have been walking around in circles for part of that, but I know that I was free from the moment I asked Jesus into my life.

I believe that there had been a different plan for my life to the one I have now. It gradually began to look more like a breaking down that was aimed at causing deliberate fragmentation possibly through the use of mind-control practices. Mind-control creates a web of deeper levels of dissociation and splits within the mind, and within these twisted webs, are laid the lies and fear that prevent the truth from being discovered. The personality fragments are like shattered pieces of glass, broken into so many shards that, with therapy alone, it would be virtually impossible to put them back together again. Fear and lies lead the child into deeper dissociation, while pain, control, and abuse cause further traumatisation and the creation of a multitude of personality states hidden in various layers and, even, mirror reflections working against each other and with each other to protect the whole system. Each fragmented personality, or alter, is trained and hidden within the layers to maintain the secret, with the front personalities hiding the deeper ones. The host personality is completely devastated and unable to make sense of the myriad of experiences going on within.

If one considers the various conspiracy theories with regards to Monarch programming, or mind-control, there is an element of this that makes sense in some of the situations we encounter. However, I don't believe we need to get drawn into a preoccupation with it and give more ground to fear. There has always been evil in this world, which manifests in a whole variety of ways, even amongst God's own believers. God is greater and bigger than all of this, and this is what we need to keep our eyes on.

I believe that the 'hypnotist' who came to the house late one night, when I was fourteen years old, had an ulterior motive other than coming to hypnotise me to make me eat. If this was a professional consultation for your extremely unwell daughter, why arrange a first consultation on an evening while they are meeting with an occult group in the room next door? He talked to me on his own initially and then told me that he was not going to hypnotise me. This had always seemed strange, even though it had come as a relief. I think however he had already 'hypnotised' me by this point, but not with the intention of making me eat but more likely to erase information from conscious recall. My dad also arranged for my sister to see a 'hypnotist,' on the suggestion that it could help cure her severe eczema, which she had had since birth. The appointment was a terrifying ordeal and did nothing to cure her eczema.

A school friend of mine told me that, when we were both five or six years old, I used to say to her that my parents were bringing me downstairs at night where a group of people would hurt me and that I was distressed about this. I would regularly tell her that I hurt in my private parts the day afterwards from what they'd done. I have no memory of ever telling her this and when she disclosed this to me, she had no knowledge of my flashbacks. She told me that she had never forgotten hearing this but didn't know what to do as a child.

After the divorce my dad joined a new group in London. I accompanied him on one occasion to an extremely opulent apartment, where I was introduced to two men who were older than my dad. We were ushered into a lavish drawing room and directed to sit at the far side while the two men completely ignored us. Dad appeared somewhat apprehensive and the men were dismissive towards him, which seemed strange if this was a regular group that he attended. I don't remember anything else about what happened, but it never made any sense as to why he took me. They seemed to have some sort of authority over him, and I can only suspect now the reason for him taking me.

People can be highly rewarded for their involvement in these organisations but those rewards are quickly withdrawn if a person wants out. Children who have been used by these type of groups will usually have been programmed for a specific reason in adulthood, whether that's for sex, or crime, or some other purpose, but which will be concealed behind a very different public persona. Unfortunately the vast majority of us don't realise the messages around us, as we defend ourselves against noticing abuse.

Whilst mind-control and child abuse may bring about complete splintering and destruction of a child's personality, God created our minds in the first place. Whatever man seeks to do through evil, darkness cannot stay dark in the light. Nothing is impossible to God and what may seem impossible to us as therapists, or doctors, or church leaders, God is omniscient—all knowing—and nothing is too difficult for Him, ever. And we, as His chosen children, are connected to Him, with full access to His shalom peace and healing. No broken personality is beyond fixing, because His word says in Colossians 1:20 (MSG)

> ...*all the broken and dislocated pieces of the universe—people and things, animals and atoms—get properly fixed and fit together in vibrant harmonies, all because of his death, his blood that poured down from the cross.*

This is God's creation, and He is in control of it no matter how powerful or evil any of these organisations think they are as they seek to infiltrate businesses and government in the same way as Nazi extremism sought to create a master race for world domination. There has always been evil in the world, but try as any might to destroy individuals, and any scheme to rise up as such a superpower, they will ultimately fail because God's plan is already determined and He already has the victory. We know the ending—God wins.

Initially when we discovered what may have happened, there was a period of deep sadness and grieving, and a fear about how it could ever be put right. I knew that God tells us to cast all anxiety upon Him because He cares for us (1Peter 5:7), and this had been a verse I had used and spoken over my life for many years. This meant that this as well could be brought into alignment with His truth because I knew that these details made no difference to anything. God had rescued me from whatever scheme had been in hand; He had reached right in and brought me out from within it—and if He created me in the first place, He certainly knew how to bring it back together again.

> *God rescued us from dead-end alleys and dark dungeons. He's set us up in the kingdom of the Son he loves so much, the Son who got us out of the pit we were in, got rid of the sins we were doomed to keep repeating. We look at this Son and see the God who cannot be seen. We look at this Son and see God's original purpose in everything created. For everything, absolutely everything, above and below, visible and invisible, rank after rank after rank of angels—everything got started in him and finds its purpose in him. He was there before any of it came into existence and holds it all together right up to this moment. Colossians 1:13–17 (MSG)*

He holds it all together. We are connected to Him, part of His vine, His body. We were created to be connected to Him, to find our purpose in Him. Nothing can prevent Him from reconnecting you to Him and completing the work He has begun in you, except you. There is no fear in Him, we are to keep our eyes on Jesus and stay close to Him on this journey, thank Him for the small things and the big things, remember His goodness and His love, and don't bother yourself with worrying about the things of this world. It will all come to an end when God determines, and we will spend eternity with Him.

I stand here now, confident in the truth of who I am as His child, confident in the truth that I am fearfully and wonderfully made, and I praise His name and thank Him for the amazing and wonderful journey we are on together. This draws me constantly closer to Him. I thank Him that He knows the answers, He knows how to heal everything, without distinction between what is physical, psychological, or spiritual, and bringing everything within us to unity, wholeness, and into His glorious light. I'm standing in the truth of that. I am not hopeless, or unloved, or without a family, because I am adopted into His family and I am secure and safe within the protection of His love.

I refuse to live my life from a victim-mentality perspective, and I choose to live it from the position of knowing that nothing is impossible for God and He will complete the good job He started in me. My body may have been trying to tell me how much it was hurting by trying to hold the weight of a terrible secret within, but this has led me deeper into a relationship with God and to understanding more of Him, His heart for us, and His love for us. He is greater than anything that was designed to destroy.

The Israelites were freed from slavery the moment God parted the waves of the Red Sea and they crossed to the other side, but they wandered around in the wilderness for forty years until they reached the Promised Land. They kept looking back and moaning about why it was taking so long, moaning about the food they had to eat, the lack of water, and saying that they would have been better off staying in slavery where they had at least been given meat to eat. God instructed them again and again to reflect on the miracles, to remember them, to focus on those things that He had done—making a way through the Red Sea, bringing water from the rock, providing them with manna to eat, etc. Then in Hebrews 12:1–3 we are reminded to keep our eyes on Jesus as we head for the finishing line and to consider what He endured for us on the cross, so that we won't grow weary and weak. Here, in this statement, is the answer for living in freedom instead of as a victim. When we're hurting and we turn to consider this, to really think about what Jesus went through for us on that cross, instead of thinking about our own problems, we cannot fail to feel better because His word states that if we do this, we won't grow weary and weak.

Whatever I went through, whatever you have gone through, whatever the horrors, the sadness, the grief, the despair, none of it is anything in comparison to what Jesus went through on the cross for us to be free. In His death, He carried the weight of the sins of the world as He hung there, the sins of all people past, present, and future—what a horrific weight that must have been. If we consider what He went through in those final moments as He gave His life as a sacrifice for us, we're released into that place of peace—we move from looking back and getting caught up in our own despair, and unto Him, and into peace.

Focusing on Jesus causes you to step into the most unbelievable incredible Shalom peace; it causes you to turn away from all distractions, misery, and pain. Looking back causes you to stumble, to be caught up in anger, regret, and bitterness. Keep your eyes on Jesus and going forwards, and you can walk free.

That doesn't mean you shouldn't have therapy because therapy involves looking back, but you do it from a place of working things out and processing it, because there is something worth fighting for. Therapy plays an important part in overall recovery and God equips and uses us to facilitate His healing—not because He needs to, but because He loves to work in partnership with us. There is a hope and a future, because in God there is always hope.

In Colossians 1:24, 26–27 Paul says:

> *[24] I can even celebrate the sorrows I have experienced on your behalf; for as I join with you in your difficulties, it helps you to discover what lacks in your understanding of the sufferings Jesus Christ experienced for his body, the church. . . .[26] There is a divine mystery—a secret surprise that has been concealed from the world for generations, but now it's being revealed, unfolded and manifested for every holy believer to experience. [27] Living within you is the Christ who floods you with the expectation of glory! This mystery of Christ embedded within us, becomes a heavenly treasure chest of hope filled with the riches of glory for his people, and God wants everyone to know it!*

He goes on to say that it was his inspiration and passion in ministry to labour with tireless intensity, with His power flowing through him, to present to every believer the revelation of being His perfect one in Jesus Christ. That's my inspiration and passion too.

I'm sharing my story with you because so many people think they can't get on with living a normal life until they are completely healed. That's so not true, or I wouldn't be doing any of what I'm doing now. You may need to take some time out at times, but basically get on with serving others and living as a free child of God now while you're working things through.

I knew that in my weakness I am strong, and that God loves to partner with us in our brokenness and turn it into something beautiful, because that brings Him glory and pleasure, and it demonstrates His enormous love for us. But, we're also created to be in partnership with others too, in the same way as we are in partnership with God—I needed Paul to stick with me and he walked alongside me in this too. As for my boys, well, we've prayed together and heard God together and part of this story has come about through some wonderful, painful, and amazing, prayer times that we have had as a family.

We've come through this as a family, with God, and we stand here together in unity, and in partnership with Him, in gratitude for all that He has taught each of us through this journey about love and faithfulness. Where God's light shines, darkness is no more and, as He has demonstrated in so many other areas of my life, here are two other examples of where He has shone His light to bring about true transformation, as only He can:

Not only is Still the Hunger, the charity, based in the very same building where I spent many hours talking to the first private psychiatrist who listened to me, which is beautifully symbolic of the vision to bridge the gap that exists between mental health and the church, but I am also now being referred patients suffering with chronic pain by the very department where I was abused by the junior doctor when I began my career in the NHS. I have a sense of God smiling at this as I help others in pain. We are working not only with those experiencing the most severe mental anguish, but also with those experiencing chronic pain. There is no distinction in my mind between emotional and physical pain as painful sensations and emotional experiences get locked within the central nervous system. Flashbacks for instance can be experienced in a whole manner of complex present-day symptoms. Sometimes it can seem impossible to determine whether the body is remembering, or whether there is a mechanical problem that needs fixing, but we do know that Jesus heals lives regardless of the background or the presentation, and His timing is always perfect.

He also healed people of their diseases and of the bad effects of their bad lives. Word got around the entire Roman province of Syria. People brought anybody with an ailment, whether mental, emotional, or physical. Jesus healed them, one and all. Matthew 4:23b–24 (MSG)